This is a true account of life at sea in the 1950's

Merchant Navy Apprentice 1951 - 1955
and the iconic shipping company 'Bank Line'

Introduction.

This book is a true account of some six years spent sailing the world as an apprentice and third officer in the iconic Bank Line. The second half is the story of how the fleet developed over 100 years, and there is also a section highlighting the Pacific adventures and ship losses suffered there post war.   The deck apprentice experience was shared by thousands of would be sailors, some who went on to greater things, and some who chose a completely different path.   This is not forgetting a similar number of engine room officers who kept the ships going in all conditions and circumstances.   Why should anyone be interested in an ordinary seagoing career?   The answer lies partly in the huge variety of ports visited, and the long voyages undertaken particularly in the Bank Line.   Each voyage was a punt into the unknown.   It was an adventure, especially for those teenagers fresh from sea school or home. A few of the ships still had European crews, drawn from the seaman's pool, and these ships suffered with drunkenness, unlike those crewed with the more serene and placid Indian crews.   The atmosphere, at work and play, was governed by the omnipresent Master, who could be kind and avuncular, but more often than not, he was someone to be respected or even feared.   It is not unfair to say that Bank Line in those 1950's years had its fair share of drunkards, tyrants, and social misfits ruling the lives of the lesser mortals on board.   This book brings out some of the nuances.

Chapters

Chapter 1....M.V. Forthbank

Life at sea began for me in the summer of 1951.   After being kitted out with an officer's uniform, complete with kid gloves, I was catapulted into a completely different world. A world of chipping and scraping, pumping up water, painting endlessly, and sleepless nights working cargo or keeping watches, and all conducted with a back drop of long boring sea passages, with luckily, much more exciting arrivals and departure from foreign ports.   The kid gloves were never used again, and they gathered mildew in the clammy tropics before being dumped over the side.   Likewise the white shoes designed to be worn with the all white and rather natty No 10 suit with the high collar.   I rather liked this kit, but had all too few opportunities to wear it.

The nautical boarding school, where I had spent 3 formative years was now behind me, but unknown to me and to the school, they had found me an apprenticeship which would prove to be priceless.   It was with a company little known outside of the shipping world, but one with 50 ships that circled the globe.   The company was the Bank Line, founded and owned by Andrew Weir, later Lord Inverforth, and looking back now it is safe to say this was an iconic British company, much respected by shipping people.   Unlike liner companies, or tramps, Andrew Weir had built up a huge and impressive network of friends and agents worldwide, all stitched together by the ships which served the various routes.   It meant that while permanent commitments were entered into, the ships were also using the charter market and tramping around where necessary. This made for an interesting life on the ships with many new and unexpected destinations, and a truly global service.

My first ship was called the M.V. Forthbank, and I joined her in Cardiff where she was in drydock. At Paddington station my tearful Mum had seen me off, emptying her purse into my hands as a last gesture of support. I was to have strong pangs of guilt when inevitably it was spent on the first pub visit. In the drydock area in Cardiff it was necessary to use shore side toilets, and being a seedy area, there were warning notices to beware, and a home made cosh hanging with the toilet key. My mind struggled madly to envisage wielding a cosh and trying to relieve myself at the same time. We were three apprentices, with me being the first tripper and the greenest! Well, you have to start somewhere. We took water through the first night alongside, and I recall sleepily pulling hoses around on the quay and aboard as we filled the fresh water tanks during the darkness. The Forthbank was an old ship, built in 1929 by Workman Clark (1928) in Belfast. She was a shelter decker, with five hatches. As a result of this design it was possible (and useful) to be able to go down into the tweendeck and walk the full length of the ship without meeting any bulkheads. Many days were sent there, either stacking, storing or removing the dunnage (timber) around, or possibly working on the giant lids to the deeptanks, secured by dozens of bolts. The Forthbank was showing her age in the accommodation where living was basic but bearable. Anyone coming from the sea school I boarded at, with its square of cheese and dry bread for supper, would find life on board this ship a doddle, however. There was no severe culture shock. Then we sailed for Trinidad where we were to load bitumen in drums.

The magic of this trip and my new life kicked in on day two. The clouds lifted, the sun shone and glinted on the water, and there was a great up-beat atmosphere around the decks. Working there in the morning, I heard a cracking sound, and looked up to see whales leaping spectacularly out of the water, and smacking their tails down hard which was producing the noise which carried across the sea. Our Chinese carpenter, a dour quiet professional, gleefully showed us flying fish which had accidentally landed on the deck in the night. As they skim from wave to wave, they occasionally ended up coming over the rail when conditions were right. The first person to pick them up was usually the carpenter whose daily duties included an early morning round of the decks, sounding the tanks and recording readings in the soundings book. Both the Indian crew and the Chinese carpenter valued the fish for drying or for frying, or sometimes curried!

The chief officer on this first ship had just survived the terrible explosion of RFA Bedenham in Gibraltar a few months earlier when 13 people were killed and many injured, and naturally enough, he was still in shock, recounting his lucky escape a few months earlier. I also recall vividly the pop tunes of the day, with Les Paul and Mary Ford belting out ' How high the moon' from the open door of the second mates cabin as we worked around the deck.

The Atlantic crossing was fairly routine, except for some concern over a leaking rivet. It was important enough for the Captain himself to get involved, and the solution was to construct a box around the leak, which was in an awkward spot, halfway up the hull in one of the empty holds. The box was filled with cement, and it did the job, temporarily stopping the inflow. The ' cement box' solution was new to me as a beginner, but over the years ahead It was used countless times and in some really odd places. It was an indispensable tool, familiar to anyone who spent time at sea.

We anchored at a place called Point Fortin, and I was to return here a few times over the years ahead. For me, it was a charming anchorage, with not much to see, other than the palm fringed shoreline, but the morning stillness, and the sparkling silent ocean, occasionally disturbed by diving birds or leaping fish, was enough to cast a spell. Mornings started cool, but warmed markedly as the sun rose. There was an air of expectancy. Our cargo came to us on barges piled high with layers of drums, and these were towed to the ship, with the sound of voices carrying distinctly across the flat surface. Before they could be loaded, slings of damp, and newly cut timber were dumped near the hatches to be used as dunnage, separating the layers and filling the void spaces as the holds filled. This dunnage had a not unpleasant, pungent smell. Our job was to get the winches working, and the derricks hoisted over the holds ready for the loading programme which went on steadily throughout the day. A steam winch is a tough piece of machinery, but the steam lines usually needed draining of hot water before the pistons flew, and the clanking sound commenced. We did this methodically opening little drain cocks under the cylinders at each hatch, closing them only when pure steam was escaping.

Interestingly, we were loading natural pitch, mainly used for road building world wide, and it came from the famous pitch lake. Sir Walter Raleigh had discovered it in 1595, and he used it first, sealing the deck on his ship in a very satisfactory way. We had an opportunity to visit the lake, which is a natural phenomena. It was hard at the edges and trenching machines were busy harvesting the tar by cutting into the semi-liquid surface . The sensation I got was similar to standing at the edge of a thawing iced over pond, where the edges only were safe. Fossilised trees and plants apparently get spewed out, and I wondered if any poor soul had ever slipped in.

Loading continued at a steady pace, and in the evenings we were able to enjoy the facilities at the nearby Shell Club. Walking up the tropical path with Cicadas croaking, and the pleasant cool air created a good feeling, made even better after a few beers. Some lads had a dip in the pool which had recently been allowed again, after a ban. This was imposed when the previous ship visitors had run amok and acted stupidly throwing all the furniture in the water.

The apprentices were detailed off to stay in the holds during loading, the idea being to monitor the stowage and prevent various shortcuts or sloppy work. It was a relatively easy task idling away chatting to the interesting Trinidadians. It was the time when steel drums were first being adapted as musical instruments and some of the stevedores enthusiastically showed me their skill. One particular man became a regular friend on this occasion and on subsequent trips when I always looked him up. He was an educated and thoughtful person who felt trapped in his life. My lasting memory is of him telling me that I had a career path and just had to keep going to achieve promotion and success, something which he envied greatly. Down the hold for long spells I learned of the dangers of standing anywhere under the hatch opening. The drums were lifted and loaded with can hooks. These simply hook on to the rims of the drums and up to a dozen could be swung into the hold, the drums rolling free as soon as the weight came off the load because the weight of the drum, over 2 cwt, kept the chains taut. The trouble came if a load nudged the hatch coating while being swung in, dislodging a hook. It happened all too often that a drum would come hurtling down to splat on the landing area, spreading a sticky mess of bitumen from the split.

Eventually we sailed for Australian ports starting with Brisbane, but first was a nearly 4 week crossing of the Pacific, entered after transiting the Panama Canal. The weeks passed quickly enough as we scraped and painted in most parts of the ship. Life as an apprentice was full of painting tasks, from inside work in the cabins and the small hospital, to the open deck and masts etc. The white gloss paint gave off an overpowering chemical smell which choked us when working in confined spaces. These were the days long before odourless paint. Islands were passed night and day, sometimes quite close, and it was my first sighting of the volcanic Marquesas islands, starting with Matu Hiva. These are part of French Polynesia, and on a route from Balboa to Brisbane, as with similar routings, it was the first island to be sighted some 12 or 13 days after leaving Balboa. Many years later, my interest in this island led me to travel books on the area, and a modern one mentions how the French community there import Perrier water from France. The island has beautiful fresh water falls, visible from seaward, so I surmised that it was the fashionable thing to do, rather than from necessity.

Being a first tripper, both me and the other lad were the victims of the traditional baiting. Being sent below to request ' a long weight' was a favourite, and it caused great amusement. It backfired however in my case, as I was suspicious of any strange sounding orders, and refused to pass on a message when berthing in Brisbane. My job was manning the telephone on the poop deck, relaying messages to the second mate below. When the bridge rang with an instruction to put out the ' Insurance wire' I laughed and ignored it, not knowing that the order was serious, and that the insurance wire was an extra heavy wire used in rivers etc. No one complained, maybe understanding my suspicion.

Chapter 2....S.S. Hazelbank

Brisbane was great, and it was my first taste of this great river city with all the delights a big city can offer.   Then we moved round the coast to Adelaide and I got a shock. Having just settled in with my new companions, I was told that I was being transferred to another ship.   For some reason, maybe to do with time left before I was due home, the head office in London had nominated me to be transferred to one of the passenger vessels which ran between Calcutta and Durban. To get there I needed to use two other ships! The first lay just along the quay no more than a few hundred yards.   She was a dirty looking coal burner, with ash piled on the deck. This was the S.S. Hazelbank, a WW2 standard built empire ship, and one which had come through the war unscathed.   I reluctantly dragged my kit along the quay, and went aboard, where I was to share a cabin with an Australian apprentice. His home was in Adelaide, and we soon hit it off, going ashore where he showed me the sights.   Some 60 years later, thanks to the internet, I was to catch up with my cabin mate, now residing in tropical Queensland, near Cairns. We also watched England play cricket at the famous Adelaide oval. So it was not all work and no play.   I recall laying out on the grass inside the Oval, with snacks and drinks, when both Edrich and Compton were batting, and the crowd good naturedly taunting Compton, who was dubbed Brylcreem boy on account of his slicked back hair.

The Hazelbank was a happy ship. It starts with the Captain, and on this ship he was a very amenable and humorous man, who joined in with the officers - a quite rare occurrence. I remember an odd thing that took place, and it concerned an exchange that the ship had with a school somewhere in the world. There were regular letters, (in those days), and the Captain took a keen interest writing. He would read out the latest epistle, and I can't be sure who started it, but the letters were full of innuendo! It would be totally politically incorrect by today's standards, but they caused no end of amusement because of the often risqué double meanings. It was stuff like

a supposed quote from a newly appointed lady teacher to the Head, who wrote, " I will be more than happy to work under you". This particular Captain also took the trouble to wish me well when he visited my next ship, the Westbank in Colombo, and called into my cabin.

We loaded bagged flour for Ceylon, and set off. Despite the fact that I had obviously ' crossed the line' when heading south for Australia, the ceremony was deemed necessary again as we sailed back north to Ceylon. It was a down market affair, with the Stockholm tar being applied to me by the Australian third mate. (see cover picture) I was lashed to the open railings by number three hatch, and smiled bravely as he wielded the brush. This ceremony has a long history, and the highlight is the arrival of King Neptune and his attendants to initiate a 'Pollywog' into the mysteries of the deep, when they then become a trusted 'Shellback'. This tradition, loved by many seafarers has a long history that goes back centuries. Maybe, I couldn't produce the vital certificate, or more likely my ceremony was an excuse to tar someone anyway.

The Hazelbank discharged most of the cargo in Galle, the port close to the famous wartime naval base of Trincomalee in the north of the island, and then it was round to Colombo. This beautiful island is most appreciated from seaward, especially when the breeze is offshore, and a lovely perfumed fragrance is in the air. On this and subsequent visits, I soaked in the distinctive atmosphere which begins with the first whiff of that spicy smell. At night, the twinkling lights of the port and city would add to the allure. In daytime, and with a strong breeze blowing, there were fast sleek catamarans racing across the surface, easily keeping pace with the ship. They looked scruffy with bedraggled lateen sails and crude misshapen outriggers, bound together, but boy, could they sail! Ashore in Colombo I first noticed the crowds all chewing betel nut and spitting all over the place. Modern hotels and restaurants were a treat, and some of us took a train out to the Mount Lavinia hotel situated further up the coast and sitting in an ideal location on a palm fringed shoreline. This hotel featured later in the ' Bridge on the river Kwai' movie when William Holden was romancing a female officer. My fellow Australian apprentice and cabin mate happened to have friends in Colombo and he kindly invited me along on a trip to Kandy, in the centre of the island. We travelled in a Morris car together and went up the twisting and spectacular mountain road through lush jungle. Saffron robed monks lined the road, and at the summit we were to see the famous ' Temple of the Tooth' where more orange robes were in abundance.

In Colombo harbour, we were moored out in the middle on the harbour buoys, and lying adjacent to another old Bank Line ship, the 'Comliebank' that we visited. The winches were racing and clanking on both, discharging bags and loading tea in chests. On board was an old friend from the Nautical School where we had shared a dormitory, and who had left a year earlier than me. We greeted each other like long lost friends. This was the end of a short sojourn on the coal burning and friendly. " Hazelbank" as I had to transfer to a newer ship arriving the following day bound for Calcutta where I could finally get on board the ' white ship' M.V. Inchanga. The arriving ship was the 'Eastbank'. Built in 1948 and a relatively recent addition, she felt a lot more businesslike straight. away. Cabins were modern, and the Doxford opposed 5 cylinder piston engine drove her along at a decent 14 or 15 knots. A sister to the similarly named West and Southbank, she had windows in her alleyways which overlooked the engine room, and when under way it was impressive watching the giant opposed piston engines, favoured by Bank Line, with their associated flexible pipes, thrashing up and down not unlike a big sewing machine.   For students of ship design and ship enthusiasts I should mention that the old world charm of the old Bank Line ships was noticeably missing. No wood decks for a start, and steel bulwarks instead of rails. This may sound trivial, but to many of us, it made a substantial difference, and the overall feeling was functional and lacking in character. For the first time in my sea going career I was on a ship with a lounge or recreation room. It wasn't much, other than a furnished space on the main deck, with comfortable chairs and a selection of books, usually provided by the Seaman's mission, but still short of later versions with bars and swimming pools which were yet to arrive on the scene.   Ship board comforts were to take a leap forward when air conditioning became the norm, but the Eastbank lacked that luxury.   There were many thoughtful improvements to arrive in the coming years, one of them being fast and manoeuvrable rescue boats transforming the task of general boat work which could only be done using big cumbersome wooden boats in my time.

The Eastbank negotiated the long journey up the Hooghly river to Calcutta, taking the best part of two days as we anchored overnight halfway up.   Then I was whisked away in a Sampan with my kit to join the ' Inchanga'.

Chapter 3....M.V.Inchanga

Arriving at the ships gangway I was still 16, and very green, but writing this many years later, the evocative spice laden smell that characterised the Inchanga is still easily conjured up.   The wide wood sheathed alleyways on the main deck had very large and low ventilator cowls, and these gave out a heady perfume of cinnamon, nutmeg, and other spices in a rich aroma. As with all perfume the intensity varied, and when the hold spaces was filled by tea chests, for instance, the familiar and pungent smell of Broken Orange Pekoe and other blends would dominate. This feature, unseen, but omnipresent, is easily the most powerful recollection for me.   I later became curious about this ship and the history of the passenger vessels   Andrew Weir, the great shipping entrepreneur, and his board

Note paper heading from the "White ship" days.

had ordered these 3 passenger cargo vessels from Workman Clark (1928) in Belfast for delivery in 1934.   It was a departure from the usual focus on their worldwide cargo services - Liner and Tramp trades, and the ships were destined for the Indian/African service, to replace the Gujarat class and ex Bucknell , Natal line ships that had been maintaining this service previously.

The terminal ports were Calcutta at one end and Capetown at the other, but it was a flexible arrangement with interesting deviations as the need arose. Durban later became the regular turn round port. A significant improvement in fittings and comfort was planned for the 50 first class passengers, and the 20 second class. Up to 500 deck passengers were also housed in the tween decks. Much was made at the time of the features for the first class which included en suite bathrooms and a glassed in tea room. Fresh water baths, not always available in pre war ship was also provided. Some sixteen years later when sailing on the Inchanga, the impression was distinctly Somerset Maugham - ish with much spacious polished wood, and a hushed and relaxed atmosphere, no doubt partly due to the relatively few passengers. The vital statistics were 7300 tons gross, length 435ft, Breadth 57ft, Draft 37ft. Twin screw 6 cylinder Workman Clark SD 60 diesels gave a speed of approx 15 knots. Before the passenger numbers were reduced many years later, these ships had 12 lifeboats with double stacking on the afterdeck. It was an awkward arrangement which called for the launching of the top boat and then the need to rewind the davits back to hook on the lower boat. The number of boats were slowly reduced over the years as the passenger capacity was changed progressively downwards.

Incomati

When the war started a few years later, there were interruptions to their intended route, and the Incomati was sadly torpedoed and sunk by gunfire off Lagos by U508 in 1943, having survived the first 4 years of hostilities. The radio officer died in the attack, but passengers, crew, and naval gunners, were eventually picked up by British destroyers. The Inchanga and the Isipingo went on to dodge the submarines and surface raiders, and had a successful 30 year career, largely running as intended between India and South Africa. The demands of war meant they occasionally deviated in those early years, joining Atlantic convoys with all the associated risks, and visiting New York and Liverpool.

Although only a few months at sea, luck or maybe bad luck, made me the senior

M.V 'INCHANGA'
MADRAS, MAY 1962

apprentice on board the Inchanga, as I was replacing an apprentice out of his time, and returning home to sit for second mate's. My cabin mate was a South African lad fresh from the highly regarded General Botha sea school. We were to become friends, and he went on to have a successful career before finally retiring as head of the South African ports organisation.

Within a few weeks, I was told that I would be acting third mate. Shock, horror! There was I still working out my ass from my elbow at 16, and I was catapulted up to the bridge deck to keep the 8 to 12 watch. In the event of course, all went reasonably well, especially as there were sympathetic fellow officers to lend a helping hand. The second mate at that time was a rare bird, who managed the Herculean task of sitting his tickets effortlessly without recourse to school. He was later to rise up to become the company superintendent for South African ports.
To set the mood of life in 1952, there is nothing better than the pop tunes of the day, and I recall that Johny Ray was all the rage, singing about ' Just crying in the rain '

and ' The little white cloud that cried'.   Other hits were Jim Reeves with ' I love you because' and Guy Mitchell with his ' Red Feathers' !

Life on board the Inchanga for me fell into a pattern. The stint as third mate lasted only briefly, when I reverted thankfully back to apprentice duties.   However, on the bridge watch there was one memorable night sailing through the Maldives Islands at night which is burned in my memory. Down below a party was in full swing, and I could hear the muted music and laughter from the saloon.   The Captain had a reputation as a lady's man so it all fitted.   On the bridge we were swooshing silently through the tropical night, phosphorescence in the bow wave, and a balmy breeze out on the bridge wing.   At this time, the Inchanga had yet to be fitted with radar, so we were sailing blind through a quite narrow passage and relying on the last star sight position, which meant that I was hanging over the bridge wing straining my eyes to see any sign of the islands or surrounding reefs. I was apprehensive in the extreme.   Events in the Bank Line fleet over the next few years more than justified my terror, as it happened.   There seemed to be a fatal attraction to the many islands we visited, lit and unlit, with consequential casualties.

Back as apprentice, a twice daily routine was the unlocking of water taps for our Asian deck passengers.   The drill was to stand by the pumps and monitor the queue.   Quite often, chickens were slaughtered by the pumps and the water used to flush the blood away into the scuppers. The chicken had its throat cut in a ritual and was then usually dumped in a wicker basket where it slowly died making croaking noises. After the initial shock of this practice it became a regular occurrence and a normal event. There was no trouble with the often large numbers of deck passengers, but there was a crush, with teeth cleaning and energetic ablutions going on in an haphazard fashion. I also remember a box on the toilet bulkhead where a queue of passengers dipped in a wet finger and then rubbed their teeth, which were usually pristine.   I was fascinated. Memory tells me this was fine sand, but on reflection, could it have been? Maybe a tooth powder.   In the tween decks they were assigned a space which was not much bigger than their bed roll, and I was amused at the way each space was regularly swept clean, but leaving the debris a few inches away from the designated area.

In the traditional way of apprentice boys we carried out a variety of tasks around the decks and in the holds, sometimes assisting the Chinese carpenter, and sometimes working alone, painting and scrapping, or servicing the lifeboats. This involved the regular replacement of the water, biscuits, and barley sugar kept under the thwarts in special tanks. Applying Stockholm tar to tanks, or setting up cement boxes was another task.   The senior apprentice received orders for the day's work from the Mate, and then it was just a matter of getting on with it.   Occasionally, it was possible to speed up the work so that the rest of the day could be free time, but it always depended on the mood and whims of the Mate. Sometimes, things went horribly wrong, as when I mistook instruction to sand down a door and revarnish it. I had found the Mate horizontal with a lady passenger when reporting to him for the afternoons work, so the mumbled instruction was understandable in our mutual embarrassment.   I then chose a highly polished door leading into the dining saloon when it had been intended to work on one of the outside doors. It had seemed odd to me, but orders were orders I reasoned!   It was only put right in Calcutta by skilled polishers, as one of a myriad of jobs on a long repair list.

We rarely mixed with the passengers, but there were moments.   Mostly, the passengers were returning or joining civil servants and sometimes they travelled with their children or relatives who were more in our age bracket.   There was one particular girl that we all fancied, including the Mate, who unfortunately for us youngsters, pulled rank.   On the main deck along the starboard side was a double cabin for the apprentices, and it was conveniently opposite the barber's shop which also stocked sweets and snacks. Never mind that the chocolates, kept in the warm were soon covered in a white deposit of unattractive mildew, we still scoffed them all when funds would allow.   Chits instead of cash facilitated this process. Next door to our apprentices cabin and separated only by a thin

bulkhead was a particularly randy and predatory electrician whose aim in life appeared to be the pleasing of any needy lady passengers. He entertained us regularly with the sounds of his energetic lovemaking.

The route from Durban to Calcutta and back took in many ports up and down the East African coast, and anchoring played a major part in our progress. Anchoring was also regularly resorted to

Ian Harvey, Apprentice, Lady passenger centre, and the author on the M.V.Inchanga boat deck.

on the Indian and Bangladeshi ports in the Sunderbans, Chittagong being the most important, where we often loaded very heavy bundles of tough, shiny, straw coloured Jute, and bales of Gunny bags for East African ports. Work went on through the night, and one of our duties as apprentices was to ensure that the gangs in the holds filled all the space right up between the beams - not an easy task. This was accomplished by many hands all working in unison to repetitive chants, not unlike European sea shanties of old, with a leader calling out and a chorus responding. It was impressive and usually carried out with good humour and diligence.   By this means, prodigious weights could be lifted up and rammed home. Lighting was provided by portable clusters as they were known, and these had a circle of bulbs for maximum effect. Keeping the bulbs replaced and re-positioning the clusters around the hold was another job for the apprentice on duty, and in a tropical downpour it could be dangerous and unpredictable as they became soaked and shorted out. Our Chinese carpenter amused us by sticking his fingers in the sockets to test for power. The Inchanga and her sister Isipingo were also designed with 4 small reefer spaces in number 4 hatch tweendeck, and these were in regular use for a variety of produce in bags. I can recall freezing nights in these spaces tallying bags in and out, whilst outside it was the lovely balmy atmosphere of a tropical night . The temptation to step outside was countered by the knowledge that pilfering or irregularities could so easily occur in our absence. It was a relief when the heavy thick doors of these lockers, as they were called, were finally slammed shut.

The longest spell at sea occurred between Colombo or Mombasa or vis versa, when a wooden swimming pool would be erected in the well adjacent to number 2 hatch, below the bridge. It was a crude, unimpressive affair, but it served the purpose and was popular with passengers and officers alike. Often, the water would slosh alarmingly from side to side as we rolled, and care was needed not to slosh someone straight over the side as the top of the pool side was slightly above the adjacent gunwale! It was a million miles away from modern pools on passenger ships.

The dining saloon had a table reserved for the apprentices and although we shared a the menu, there were occasions when certain items were off limits to us and reserved solely for passengers. Getting out of working gear, and into whites in order to eat in the saloon was also a bind, and we preferred to eat outside if it was possible.

Arriving and leaving port my role was assisting the Mate on the Foc'sle, and I had personal charge of the wooden painted anchor buoy which served such a useful role in fast flowing muddy waters. This was simply a float attached to an anchor fluke by thin wire, and coiled up and secured on the rail with sail twine ready for use. When the anchor flew out, the twine lashing broke, and the buoy would usually give us a tell tale location of the anchor on the bottom. It was a rough and ready tool which often went wrong but it was useful in the main. I learned a lot in that year about anchoring, and the fascination for a youngster like me at that time was the variety of trash that came up on the flukes. Everything from other people's anchors, i.e. those from nearby ships, to ropes and wires, and debris of all sorts. When the windlass started straining loudly, I knew we had caught a big one! Washing tons of mud from the flukes with a hose was part of the fun. It also happened that we often needed to unshackle the anchor to attach the chain to river buoys in some of the ports served.

On the African coast, we usually had a leisurely stop in Mombasa, where the pace of life in the port was slow and measured. It was the days when the British India's shipping company had the lovely Kampala and Karanja in port and we might easily be on the next berth dwarfed by their size and opulence. It also meant time for relaxation, playing table tennis in the seaman's mission, or a trip up Port Reitz in the motor lifeboat when we swam and drank beer in the Port Reitz hotel. Looking back, I also recall loading bags of raw asbestos from the inland mines, long before the warnings were sounded over the dangers of this material. Further down the coast, stops were made at Zanzibar and Dar Es Salaam, and often in the minor port anchorages of Linda, Tanga, and Pemba. It was idyllic but short stops meant constant anchoring and stopping and starting. Beira was a major call, and strangely we often suffered the dreaded wait for a berth, anchoring off in the bay. This seemed strange, because our passenger status and network of agents usually ensured that we were able to ' jump the queue '. Not here though, and I recall working on deck in sweltering heat and being bitten by Tsetse flies which could easily sting through the shirt. Next stop south would be Lourenço Marques, now Mobutu, and these two ports were pleasant stops with great local beer often served up with a variety of snacks including beans.   They were railway ports with tracks coming down to the quay with copper bundles and other produce.

At Durban, a bit further down the coast, we ended the run and started loading for the long trip back to Calcutta.   Durban was a great port, the seafront hotels and bars looking most welcome from seaward, especially at night with all the magical twinkling coloured lights.   The port is marked by the famous Bluff, a headland guarding the entrance channel, and this represented home, or as near as we could get to it.   We often had valuable transshipment cargo to discharge and our job as apprentices was to remain down the holds to try and prevent pilfering.   Silks and clothing from Japan were in bundles, and I recall fashionable shoes packed in boxes with the left ones together, and the corresponding shoes in separate cartons, presumably to also deter pilfering.   On one occasion during one of my stints in the hold, the labourers, always in great fettle, laughing and singing, crammed two left shoes on their feet. Then they climbed out of the hold at the end of the shift dressed in gaudy silk scarves and dresses, still laughing and singing, and attempted to run the gauntlet of the strict dock guards. It was hard not to admire their temerity and their high spirits.

At the other end of our approx 12 week run was Calcutta and a special life for several weeks. Special and different because that was where running repairs were carried out, also drydocking if due, and the intensity and vibrancy of Calcutta meant life was generally disrupted like it or not. Arriving in the brown and sometimes turgid waters at Sandheads, where the Hooghly river discharges into the Bay of Bengal, the first sight would be a gaggle of ships anchored and waiting for a berth. Any delay here would be short, and we would take a pilot for the long and tortuous route up to the city.   The pilotage was always a challenge due to the ever changing mud banks, and we usually anchored halfway overnight before proceeding. Starting either in Kiddapore or King George docks, we would then shift out to the river buoys to load.   More often than not, it was necessary to strengthen the moorings to cope with the bore tide which is a feature of the Hooghly, bracing ourselves for the surge of water as the incoming tide overcame the normal outflow. Carcasses in the river were a common sight, including the occasional human. Often a hawk would be perched on the bodies, as they flowed silently downstream. If a drydocking was on the cards, life could be seriously disrupted as trips to shoreside toilets became necessary, and the hammering, banging and sometimes riveting invaded the peace. Trips ashore in the evening meant negotiating the hordes of youngsters with their had outstretched chanting the regular mantra "one Anna, One Anna, One Anna." Despite all this, I have fond (ish) memories of the time, walking past compounds with lilting Indian music in the air, along with the fire smoke, Up in the main street of Chowringhee, life teemed with roadside barbers and hawkers offering all sorts of goods and personal grooming like massages and ear clearing. Here on a memorable day in 1952, I saw 'Singing in the Rain' with Gene Kelly, and for an hour or so I was transported to another world a million miles from the daily bustle on board ship. It was magic at the time. There was also a great open air bar with cabaret which had the same effect on me. Looking back, I must have been a bit fragile.

Chapter 4....M.V. Westbank

Eventually, after my time away rose to 18 months, someone back in head office

 decided that I would leave the Inchanga in Durban for a trip home co-incidentally on the M.V. Westbank, again.   She had just been dragged off of the island of Juan De Nova in the Mozambique Channel where she had run up an unlit beach in the night. It was touch and go, but the salvage eventually succeeded and she was towed down and patched up in Durban.   Huge steel girders were welded along the side at bilge keel level, and for good measure she was then loaded with a full cargo of Manganese ore for discharge in Immingham.   Not a cargo usually associated with a damaged ship, but the necessary clearances would have been obtained.

We had a fairly uneventful trip home. The atmosphere was muted, in accordance with officers and crew still trying to come to terms with how they had run her up the beach in the night. Stories of how the grounding had affected the various officers were eagerly listened to by me, as I always have had a fascination for ship disasters. It seems that the salving by a B.I. tug was a difficult process and she was lucky to be dragged off eventually. There were to be a few other groundings by the companies ships that ended in disaster over the next few years, partly due to our affinity with Pacific Islands.   At the subsequent company enquiry for the

Westbank grounding on Juan De Nova, midway in the Mozambique Channel, it was established that a very strong current was to blame. The Chief Officer on watch at the time, had just finished working his morning sights, and the results were so at odds with the expected position they were disregarded or seriously doubted. In fact they were accurate. Some years later I was to sail again with the chief officer in another of the company's ships, when he was Master and I was Mate. Understandably, he had a great aversion to unlit islands. Another gem from the enquiry was the verbal examination of the Indian lookout stationed in the bow. It appears that he had seen the island and the shore looming up ahead but had not rung the warning bell on the forecastle, because the island was unlit, and as he saw it, his job was to report lights!

The January that we came up into the Western approaches, was a bad one for weather. Fog came down and we felt our way eerily past Ushant with the fog horn blaring out every two minutes as stipulated in the rules. We apprentices were working on deck painting lifebelts I recall, and everything was wet from the fog, and this combined with the harsh note of the fog horn created gave a strange detached feeling. We were aiming for Immingham, one of the bleakest ports in England, and particularly so at 3am on a freezing morning. The memory still lingers!

So ended my first trip in the Bank Line. It had taken in 5 ships and lasted nearly 20 months, which included the fascinating spell on the unacknowledged flag ship of the company. Maybe this title would be disputed by all the M.V.Isipingo veterans. However, what is not in dispute is that like all voyages in the Bank Line, it was not so much a routine trip, but more like a full blown adventure.

Chapter 5....M.V. Ernebank

In 1953, after a spell of leave, I then joined another old timer, M.V. Ernebank in Bromboro Dock, Birkenhead.   She was built in 1937, and had come through WW2 to have many more post war trading years.

 It was a memorable voyage around the world which lasted eight months and took in both the Panama and Suez canals, and in the process, considerably advanced my education.   She was a stately looking vessel to my eyes, with a long wood sheathed foredeck, of Oregon pine, and open rails. It was a voyage with quite a few ' firsts ' for me, an eighteen year old apprentice, still not quite dry behind the ears!   There were three of us, a tough looking Aberdonian, who was actually a gentle character, and who was to become a good friend, and a first tripper from Bearsden, near Glasgow.   Our stay in Birkenhead was extended as we drydocked after discharge, probably for a 15 year survey.   The trip was a riot from the start as we guzzled up to 12 pints a night in the pubs of Birkenhead - something I had never done before.   I also discovered New Brighton pier and dancehall, which burned down in later years, and where huge crowds jived to loud music and where the darkened balcony was a convenient place for dozens of snogging couples. It was a foretaste of the ' swinging sixties," still to come.   My new friend from Aberdeen led the way, and to finish off we usually found some local girls to walk home. This lifestyle was a revelation to me, and it was only a small taste of promising things to come.

The Ernebank was a typical pre-war Bank Line ship with 5 hatches, and rather pleasing but unpretentious lines, built by Harland and Wolf in Belfast, 431ft long, with a four cylinder Burmeister & Wain diesel engine giving her a decent 13 knots. Built as a shelter deck vessel, with the normal small tonnage hatch aft, she enjoyed the advantage of reduced dues on account of her low measured tonnage of 5388 net.

We were discharging Copra and valuable coconut oil, and it was a regular feature of the Bank Line trading pattern which brought their ships back to the UK and the end to what were often very long voyages. A few ships enjoyed 'short' 6 to 8 months voyages on a more or less regular basis, and these were christened 'Copra ships.' They were much sought after by some, but by no means all of us!

The first sight of the ship, rounding the quayside shed in a taxi, always gave me a thrill. It was a mixture of apprehension and pride. Never mind that the hull might be a bit rust streaked or that the gangway looked rickety, it was home for possibly 2 years, the length of the articles. The familiar sound of steam winches, hissing and clanking as they worked was music to my ears. The deck was cluttered with hatch boards, steel beams, and a variety of repair pipes and hoses, and even this sight felt comforting in a strange sort of way. There would also be a rich pungent smell of coconut oil, which was being pumped ashore with temperature raised to keep it liquid and flowing. On board, the first task was to locate my cabin and meet new shipmates. What would they be like, and who is the all important Captain who would play God for the foreseeable future?

Conditions on board were once again basic, if not primitive. Air conditioning was yet to be fitted on ships, so we relied on simple fans, with oscillating ones being much prized. Metal scoops were jammed in the port openings to catch any air, and in port it could be stifling, especially at night. Fresh water had to be pumped by hand, and was strictly rationed. The apprentices were charged with topping up the washing water for the officers as well as for their own use. It happened occasionally that water needed to be pumped from the forepeak, rather than the small domestic tanks amidships, and this was no mean feat at sea when there was a seaway running. I can still remember struggling forward, buckets in hand, the deck often glistening in the wet, and descending down the forepeak hatch to swing on a semi-rotary pump. The other apprentice stood by the buckets on deck and was supposed to call down when the job was done. There were occasions when relations were not good and he simply walked away leaving me pumping!

We sailed down the Mersey finally, and I was on the forecastle watching the Liver birds slowly coming in line. My journey began at this point, and ended as they lined up on return. It was my private little world. This was to be a very happy ship, with no dissension, and great camaraderie, which was not always the case.

First stop was Cuba, to load bagged sugar. As we left UK waters, I had my familiar feeling of euphoria. A couple of days out, the grey skies lightened, the sun beamed down, and any gloom vanished as if by magic.

The loading ports were along the south coast, starting with Manzanilla in the Granma province of Cuba. Castro had yet to wrestle control of the country, so it was the hedonistic Cuba of Batista that we were to sample. Free enterprise and western decadence flourished, including gambling dens in the capital, Havana. Here we all ended up in a bordello - my first. My companions from the ship believed in the ' work hard, play hard' school of life, and they led the way. Inside there was a sort of bar and dance hall with benches round the sides and typical rhythmic Cuban music blaring out. Dodgy looking characters, other than our party that is, were sitting around or or leaning on their partners on the dance floor. Some had towels round their waists. It was an era of fantastic sounds which I privately called ' chop chop' music on account of the hypnotic beat. The ' ladies' of the establishment were mostly care worn, to put it politely, but they looked somewhat better after we had downed a few glasses of rum. The locals drank it straight out of the bottle. Next stop was a captivating little town called San Ramon.

It had a single jetty which we tied up to, and this had a single track railway running down from the factory on high ground behind the town. The procedure was that loaded trucks were despatched from the factory, and ran down the hill by gravity, controlled only by a man perched on top with a crude screw down brake. He often looked terrified, and for good reason as accidents were common, and a man was unfortunately killed during our period loading. This led to a day of mourning. When the ship was back loading, the trucks thundered through the centre of the little town, where chickens and children scattered on hearing the approach. We sat drinking the potent white rum of Cuba at the bar tables either side of the track and watched the pantomime, fascinated.

When we were full, around the 10,000 ton mark, we sailed for New Orleans, a very short journey, and probably the shortest trip I would ever make with a fully loaded cargo. After the long run up the Mississippi, we tied up in Algiers to discharge, on the far bank of the river from New Orleans. Canal street, was easily reached, however, where we could find the Walgreens and Walmart stores. Here was an opportunity to stock up with all sorts of items. For me, it was the great 'Sea Island' cotton khaki shirts and pants which were such good quality. Also mundane things like heavy duty fishing line for the Pacific stops. Fishing was popular with all on board, and there were many occasions around the islands when we enjoyed the bonus of watching the fish take the bait, often deep down when the water was perfectly clear. When we stopped temporarily at sea for the engineers to carry out an essential repair, the lines went straight over to see what might be caught. We never knew the variety and size of the catch, which could be enormous and stretch the full length of a bathtub. It always puzzled me how the crew seemed to know which species were safe to eat, or desirable.

Then, surprisingly, after discharge, it was back over to Cuba for a full load of sugar, this time for Japan. We loaded this time on the north side of the island, way offshore, almost out of sight of land. Here there are large groups of smaller islands, and we anchored to receive the sugar from barges. It was a port for Caibairen, the main town a short way inland, and we lay at anchor in crystal clear water, teeming with fish. Due to the very warm nights, we decided as apprentices to sleep on deck under the stars, and we set to, making folding canvas bunks which worked brilliantly. During this stay at anchor, the coronation of the present Queen took place. The time difference with the UK meant that it was early in the morning for us, and our Scottish nationalist engineers all gathered around the radio hoping to hear about a possible interruption that had gathered credence, when the famous Stone of Scone would be recovered for Scotland. They were disappointed.

The stevedores offshore were the toughest I have ever seen, and they were mostly bow legged, which I imagined was from the work staggering round the holds with the sacks of damp brown sugar, each of which weighed 2 cwt. At lunchtime a boat would deliver beer in crates, and many of the workers fished for their lunch. I recall seeing them remove the beer caps with their teeth, and some actually bit into live fish as they came over the rail. It was an amazing sight, which I have never seen since. This stop was also the place where I became seriously ill with too much white rum. We went ashore in a launch and returning to the ship, I was helpless on the deck, vomiting and defacating simultaneously , while the workers, many with their lunch boxes perched on their knees, watched in amusement. It was beyond drunk, and I have never touched rum in all the years since.

The author and the senior apprentice playing chess.

We transited the Panama Canal, and early on in the Pacific voyage to Yokohama. the Captain, who was a real gent from the Shetland Islands showed us apprentices how to make fudge from brown sugar. He was a true seaman who could snap sail twine with his beefy hands, and he encouraged us lads in many ways, passing on his considerable knowledge.   For the fudge, we ' found' some sugar from the holds, and the technique was to simply mix in condensed milk using big tin trays placed on the galley stove. The end product could be hard and brittle, or soft and bendy, depending on the time over the heat.

The ship was painted down during the 4 week crossing, the usual procedure away from the hustle and bustle of life in port.   I also taught my Aberdeen friend how to play chess, which we did sitting out on deck.

Yokohama was heaven. We lay at anchor in the bay, and the winches clattered away 24/7 as we discharged through the night with lights. Ashore can only be described as a paradise for us youngsters.   I can still recall the name of the particular bar which we made home. It was called 'Bar 9 of Hearts', probably long gone, but here we found beautiful willing girls whose job it was to entertain us.   We played card games, mostly strip poker, for fun, and a great time was had by all. Japan was only 8 years out of WW2, and the American occupation was very evident, creating a fascinating mixed western and oriental atmosphere.   Kobe, and the big port of Moji were the other discharge ports, but our thoughts stayed with Yokohama where we had enjoyed ourselves so much. Our ship board duties meant that my fellow apprentice and I reluctantly had to share our imagined romance with the same girl on alternate nights!   It's tough at sea.   There were more trips to ' Girlie houses' in Kobe, the second engineer leading the charge. As the comedian of the party, he led the way, we arrived at a particular venue he had chosen where we were ushered into a reception room with drinks laid out. As the spokesman he said " not now, ". Then, after a pause, " In five minutes", when the Madam of the place politely asked us if we wanted girls to join us for drinks. Some of our other antics are best left out of this narrative!   These bars or girlie houses were very common at the time, no doubt because of the large number of American military still in residence. There was one embarrassing and cringe worthy episode when we chose our partners for the night, only for the kitty to come up short. We were asked to wait outside in the hope that better offers would come along. I had taken a strong fancy to a very attractive young girl, and she was keen for us both to disappear into the night, but it wasn't to be.

Before leaving Japan we bought all the new gadgets freshly available, like the novel transistor radios of the time, and binoculars for bridge work. It was the post war period in history when Japanese goods were shoddy, the lenses falling out of the binoculars, or worse. We still bought them however, and I cherished a little black leather covered Sony transistor that kept me in touch with the world for months. It sat snug in the porthole, held tight by the weight of the heavy brass port itself.

Word came through that we were to load Copra for home. It was to be a short trip after all. Elation by some, but we still had to go through the slow and tortuous process of trawling round the Pacific islands loading. The

Near the summit of a dormant volcano in Rabaul. Author on the right .

sequence of ports to visit included Honiara in the Solomon Islands, the scene of heavy fighting by the American troops in WW2, and Gizo. The island of Samari, where it was possible to walk right around easily, and finally Rabaul in East New

Britain. We commenced the necessary hold cleaning, which was mainly sweeping and bilge clearing, and this was carried out by the Indian crew and Chinese carpenter, plus the Apprentices.

All went well in our island hopping, with some unconventional berthing to suit the local conditions, including the use of a convenient tree stump. In Rabaul, we tied up alongside the hull of a wreck, which became officially the ' wreck berth' for many years, and as the name suggests, it was the levelled top of a sunken vessel, one of dozens littering the big harbour. Signs of the fierce fighting was everywhere, although some 8 years had elapsed. The glint of crashed aluminium Japanese fighter planes could be seen high up in the jungle, and we trekked up to have a closer look. In a moment of madness we also chose to climb a prominent volcano overlooking the port, and this took our party through cultivated fields of pineapple plants.

Rabaul residents are famed as great drinkers, and we fell in with the Australian stevedores who seemed to party at every opportunity, and some. This interesting town, pictured with the volcano in the background, was to be completely covered in ash and severely damaged much later due to a volcanic eruption. There were some bizarre moments during our stay when I staggered back across fields in the dark after excusing myself from a heavy session. I could see the port in the distance, but a garish, very noisy, and colourful event stood in my path. Maybe it was my tipsy state, but UFO sprang immediately to mind. I was in pitch black surroundings, wading through quite long grass. It was a bit scary, not knowing what might be lurking. As I drew closer, I realised it was my first view of some captivating Chinese opera being staged largely for the sizeable Chinese community in Rabaul. I loved it immediately, and have been hooked ever since.

After a number of weeks we had completed loading. It was my first experience among the charming New Guinea people with their amazing pidgin language which we were eager to mimic.   'Shoot lamp' for a torch was my favourite expression. They were also great exponents with a fishing spear, and we would watch fascinated while they expertly fished around our berths.

Before sailing for the Red Sea and home, the Ernebank bunkered at Balikpapan in Borneo. Here we were sold spirits from the bum boats, labelled Whiskey, Gin, and Rum, but in reality all the bottles contained the same strong spirit. Only the labels were different.   We drank it anyway.

In the Red Sea, steaming up towards the Suez Canal, there was a following wind for a long period. This created a still atmosphere on board in which the tenacious Copra bugs flourished.   These little black Beatles thrive wherever there is coconut, and we were heavily infested. They were in the bread which necessitated holding slices up to the light to pinch out the offenders, and they got everywhere. This habit became automatic, and stayed with me for years afterwards. We amused ourselves by dropping them in buckets of water, but they merely sank to the bottom and walked out up the sides. It was hard not to marvel at them.   When it was particularly unbearable, the ship steamed around 360 degrees, which had the effect of blowing millions of them off in a big black cloud as we came up into the wind.

The passage home went smoothly otherwise, and after transiting the canal at night, we passed through the Mediterranean Sea and onwards to the Mersey. The cargo of oil and Copra was destined for the Lever Bros plant in Birkenhead, and we anchored in the centre of the Mersey for the formalities, 8 months out.   I saw the Liver birds slowly come into line as we steamed past, marking my silent completion of the round trip. Because we had been in Japan, the customs rummager's took a particular interest in our declarations.   In my case I had a lot of goods, too many to declare, and including a bolt of Shantung silk which my dear old Mum had requested. What to do about declarations?   Most of us spirited away the offending items to favourite hiding places in the time honoured fashion.   I craftily chose the space below the saloon seats where the Customs team were sitting. It was a great inspiration, and worked perfectly. You could say they kept my stuff warm for me, but there was a snag. When the time came for me to say goodby and depart, they were still sitting, chatting, while I fretted outside. Eventually, I did make it home, and a few days later a full box of Aberdeen kippers arrived at the door, a kindly and generous gift from my recent shipmate.

Like all voyages in the iconic Bank Line, this had been an adventure that could not have been bought. With the passage of time, it has become clearer to me how lucky and privileged I was to have enjoyed such an experience.

Chapter 6....S.S. Maplebank

In the fleet in the 1950's were a number of Liberty Ships, and these were a quite
different experience to sail on. The ports and the random voyages stayed the same,
but the accommodation layout and facilities, much improved on regular old time
Bank Boats, meant that the company chose to crew them with Europeans.   One
such was the S.S. Maplebank, ex Samwash, and she was a lovely lady.   A bit

 bedraggled, and maybe a bit
over worked, but a lady none the
less.   To start with, the American
build gave the liberty ships
superior fittings, wider bunks
with proper bunk boards instead
of slats, running hot and cold
water in each cabin, and a

heating system to die for.   This particular ship had been present at the war
landings in Sicily some 10 years earlier .   After a longish spell of leave I received
the usual terse telegram to join the S.S. Maplebank.   Lolling around at home
between these trips and the adventures they offered was always an anti-climax for
me, the reason being that the long voyages did not enable any friendships, or girl
friends, for that matter.   People lose interest fast when you go away for 2 year
stints.   The Bank Line was notorious, in my eyes at least, for minimum contact.
They would easily have won the booby prize in any contest entitled " Know your

staff". Consequently, although committed 101% to the company, exchanges with the head office boiled down to a bog standard short telegram with joining instructions. Occasionally, I tripped up to Bury St London, unable to bear the silence. The experience was slightly surreal as I climbed the stairs and entered the silent thick carpeted reception area with frosted glass and asked timidly to talk to someone. Then followed a 15 minute conversation in which various ships would be mentioned as possibles for the next voyage, but the precise one depended more on schedules and positioning rather than any preference on my part. It was always very polite, if a bit distant. Looking back, I am amazed I never had the gumption to request an early return to sea, but dragged out the leave period in full. This coy characteristic seems to dog seafarers as I had a good friend and long time Master in the Bankline in later years. His fondest wish was to serve ashore in a superintendent capacity, and after some years without the call, I asked him if he had actually asked or told people in authority what his ambition was. No, was the baffling answer.

Once again, it was back to Bromboro Dock, and the Maplebank. The route via Lime Street station was a familiar one, and soon I was in a taxi eagerly looking for that first glimpse of my new home for the next 2 years. I knew vaguely that the Maplebank was a war built ship, but it was to be my introduction to the now famed Liberty ship, or ' Sam boat' as they were called. It was winter still and as luck would have it, onboard repairs meant that the heating on board was shut down. With no hot food either, we all trooped over to the Lever Bros canteen in the dock for meals. She was discharging Copra and coconut oil from the deep tanks and once again the distinctive and evocative smell gave me a comforting feeling. Mentally, I was home. On board, the apprentices cabin that I was to occupy was on the bridge deck, and I was amused to see a cosh dangling from the cabin radiator. This, together with a heavy steel door at the bottom of the companionway was explained away as necessary on this, a " White crew" ship, with all that was supposed to mean. We had yet to meet the deck crew, but when we did, it was the start of a hilarious and eventful experience. Liverpool crew's, which they were, can be immensely humorous and funny, even in odd circumstances, and so it proved. The humour wore a bit thin on occasions when, later in the voyage, we had to cover for their drunken absence. They were mostly true seamen, capable of all the skills needed, and in spare moments at sea, they sewed themselves working clothes from duck canvas carried on board. This included a ' cheese cutter ' cap to finish off. The bosun, who was a big man with light blue piercing eyes, earned beer money by fashioning natty little sailing ships on a varnished base utilising chicken carcasses from the galley. A couple of the young deck boys still were unable to read properly, and later in the voyage, we apprentices occasionally read their letters out loud to them.

The chunky design of these American built vessels appealed strongly. Everything was that more robust, and good quality. Bunks were wider, heating was powerful, layout was generous, and overall it was a great experience sailing around in them. On the bridge was basic equipment like steering console, telegraphs, echo sounder, etc, and there was an upper bridge with the compass relayed optically. Up on top, where we steered most of the time in the tropics, a small raised timber structure served as a wheelhouse, and it often happened on this voyage that I not only steered, but rang the telegraph and blew the whistle when in pilotage waters. It was like something straight out of the tales of the T.V. show, Para Handy, on the ' Vital Spark' a Clyde puffer!

The familiar design of the 'Sam boats' as they were known included gun bays on the fore side of the bridge structure, and although the guns were long gone, the bays served as handy lookout positions, and could vibrate alarmingly when steaming into a gale of wind. This happened noticeably later in the voyage, when we were passing through the Cook Strait in New Zealand.

After crossing the Atlantic in ballast, the Maplebank commenced her loading pattern along the U.S. Gulf ports. First stop Galveston in Texas for the rock sulphur base cargo. As usual the yellow rock and powder was poured into the holds, and levelled over by bulldozers to provide a platform for the heavy farm machinery to come. We witnessed the impressive blue flashes as the dust ignited from sparks. Timber boards went down, and lashing gangs with typical American efficiency, and ample tools, plus reels of shiny new wire would lash the vehicles securely in place. It was a very common thing in Bank Line however, that despite what looked like secure lashing, we often had to risk life and limb at sea, trying to stop breakaway machinery. Heavy rolling would nearly always loosen the lashings and in the worst case the giant harvesters or tractors would rush from side to side threatening to damage the hull plating.

Galveston was always a treat with it's easy style, western music, cold beer and juke boxes. The stores were a magnet for me also with such good quality working gear. We proceeded up the Mississippi again and to the berth where there was a regular parade of Bank Line ships, one a week was normal. I had long stints at the wheel, and enjoyed every minute of it. It was during one of these spells at the wheel that I had the first of what is called a life changing moment. It wouldn't be the last. The sight of the Mississippi pilots in their coloured shirts, confident manner, and with their efficient self assurance impressed me greatly. Here was a possible career path that I could envisage aiming for. What more could a man want? The berth we occupied was called Harmony St wharf, and it was a wooden structure on the river. Here, the dockside, just below the quay level, was festooned with wooden plaques bearing the flag and name of earlier ships. Many were a work of art, and we added a suitable one, crafted by the apprentices and crew. Slogans were common, along with the necessary ship and name and date of the visit. While we lay there, a large heavy lift refinery tube weighing 50 plus tons was lifted onto the afterdeck by a floating crane. The crew dubbed it " Kon Tiki " and painted this on it in large letters.   I can't imagine the receivers in New Zealand, where we were bound, would be too pleased.   After rounding up the crew ashore and completing the loading, we sailed for Cristobal and the Panama Canal transit. Here we had a crisis. Arriving in the evening, it was quite magical.   The twinkling lights of the port and the city, the soft warm humidity, and the relaxing atmosphere of a quiet anchorage out in the harbour all added to the feeling of well being. Boats came and went, and it was all too easy for the deck crew to get ashore to enjoy the local delights.   Off they all went. A few engineers also took the opportunity to explore the delights of the Cristobal bars, and somehow there was a fracas during the evening resulting in one of them getting stabbed, though fortunately not a fatal stabbing. Our Canal Transit was set for 6am, but no crew had returned. It was decided to set off anyway, the apprentices manning the wheel, and a scratch crew of officers and apprentices dealing with the necessary rope and wire handling for the mechanical mules that were a feature of the canal, accompanying the ships in and out of the locks.

I steered from the topside position and we set off. The pilot's walkie talkie crackled all the way through the Canal, and I was able to hear a running commentary on the rounding up of our wayward crew. Every time there was a capture, it was relayed to the ship!   All good fun, I thought.   A discussion took place over the radio, when it was decided to send all the crew through to Balboa at the Pacific end of the canal by train.   After passing through the fresh water lakes, where we topped up our tanks, we exited under the bridge at Balboa, and anchored in the Bay.   Topping up tanks with free fresh water in the Lakes when transiting the Panama Canal was a regular feature, and a perk, if you like.   This practice has now been banned, I believe.   A police launch appeared after a while bringing the merry makers reluctantly back.   I was at the top of the pilot ladder to assist, and saw they were handcuffed before being allowed to ascend the ladder. Once on deck, a couple of them searched around, and hurled wedges and loose shackles back down on the boat, but the police had had enough and just sped away.

In those days, it was common for crew to be fined by the Master. The usual punishment was forfeiture of a days wages for discipline breaches, and the person being fined was able to choose a charity from a list to receive the money. The Bosun and his men with their usual humour claimed they had opted for ' The

Destitute Master Mariners club. ' when we spoke to them in the morning. There was never any regret or apology about their behaviour. It seemed to be taken for granted that every opportunity should be taken to enjoy circumstances where drink could be obtained. Whatever the scenario however, I never saw our Liverpool shipmates without a great sense of humour.

So after the Canal, we set off on the long 2 week voyage across the wide Pacific Ocean. Although it looks empty, it is actually dotted with clusters of islands, and some quite remote single ones which, for me at least, made this period welcome and interesting. The normal practice on this stretch was to paint the ship, more or less all over, and this we did, joining up on deck with our now sober crew. During this process, someone got detailed off to climb to the top of the masts, and work their way down painting as they went. The tallest mast being the thin t'gallant which was peculiar to the Liberty ships. This top section only served as a signal mast but it doubled as a convenient hoist for my radio aerial at sea. Looking at groups of ships from afar, say at an anchorage, it was also easy to identify Liberty ships as a result of this feature.

On this long ocean voyage, a chess tournament was organised, and much to my surprise and slight embarrassment, I managed to beat the Chief Officer at a match in his cabin. The silence at the end was deafening.   Another rather popular activity was ' horse racing' arranged on an after hatch under lights.   Dice were rolled to determine the moves of the horses and everyone including the Captain and Chief Engineer joined in.   A crossing the line ceremony was also arranged for the new sailors, and a pool constructed. Our Liverpool crew were quite innovative and made elaborate costumes plus the almost mandatory trident for King Neptune.

Once tied up in Auckland, and in all the discharge ports thereafter , the shenanigans by the boozy crew re-commenced - sometimes hilariously, and sometimes not so. A pub piano was 'borrowed' and hoisted aboard in Lyttelton to much jollity and rejoicing, and come sailing time, I was usually nominated to visit all the dockside or town pubs to persuade or cajole the deck crew to return, not always successfully.   Littleton was a cosy little port, and it nestles in the big crater of an extinct volcano from long ago.   Hills surround the town and port, and being young and adventurous a couple of us decided to climb up the face of the steepest one. There was a shock at the summit when we found people picnicking on the top. Unbeknown to us a road ran up the reverse side from Christchurch. Visiting the pubs at sailing time and locating our crew usually led to some good natured banter mixed with the usual F... offs.   I often returned to the ship empty handed. In the worst situation, the apprentices and some of the officers were forced to close the hatches, lower the derricks, and sail the ship. It didn't end there, because often there was no one sober enough to take the wheel, so it fell to us apprentices again. One night after a particularly long spell at the wheel, I requested a relief, and up came an AB who took the wheel unsteadily as I scootered down the ladder. As I did so there was a crash, and I looked round to see him collapsed in a heap.   - Happy days!

As we progressed around the coast there were gaps in our ranks. In those days it was not such a heinous crime to 'jump ship' and the authorities were more lenient with the deserters. Many of our crew stayed in NZ and Australia and made a good life for themselves. There were plenty of vacancies for bar staff, taxi drivers, and in the building trade which was booming. The Master in these cases appealed to the Agent ashore, who together with the police usually brought replacements down, and these were often crew who had deserted from other ships and who had been rounded up, and sometimes brought to the gangway in handcuffs. It was a sort of merry-go-round whereby any of our crew caught would likely be taken to the next ship losing crew. During this period, the Maplebank got nominated by the company for the well known but dreaded ' phosphate run'. It was the short straw of places to go. This involved sailing up in ballast to either Ocean Island, or Nauru, both near the Equator. We then loaded phosphate rock for discharge in either Australia or New Zealand, where it was a valuable land fertiliser. The round trip was around 4 or 5 weeks or even longer depending on the facilities and the rate of discharge at the civilised end! The bad news was that once on this run, it was normal to do several trips before being released to more adventurous and interesting pastures.

On Ocean Island there was a small ex pat community, and we played them at both cricket and football. Due to the land formation and the method of extraction of the phosphate rock, the terrain around the cricket pitch consisted of deep pock marked gullies where the ball would disappear for good. It all added to the fun. It also relieved the monotony of the daily on board routine. There was a recently wrecked Bank Line ship sitting close to the shore, and in two pieces apart from a strip of plating. She was the " Kelvinbank", another Liberty vessel like ourselves, and she had had a bit of bad luck, getting afloat after temporarily grounding, only to get stuck on the remains of an earlier wreck in the 1920's called the ' Oomah'. That was the end for the Kelvinbank which broke up ino pieces in the following years. It was a spectacular sight, and we took a few photos. Some of the crew attempted to board to obtain souvenirs but she had already been stripped bare.

At nearby Nauru, the rock was loaded somewhat faster, being shot into the holds from purpose built loading arms.   We swam from the ship, but due to a short loading period there were no exploratory trips ashore. So, up and down we went, the route necessarily taking us through the notorious Tasman sea, which often produced storm conditions with accompanying sea and swell. As a youngster it was fun, just like most things, and although the Liberty ships were great vessels, there were a few recorded incidents worldwide of severe cracks appearing under stress. Fortunately, these were mainly blamed on very cold conditions, but sitting on the poop in very rough weather marvelling at the slight flexing that was visible looking forward, it never occurred to me that there may have been any danger.   My stints at the wheel were a regular thing and in very heavy weather, more

 concentration was needed not to get thrown off course.   On one occasion, thumping into the swell with resultant waves washing down the foredeck, the Captain's wife appeared on the bridge, and after studying the conditions, she called the Captain saying, " I think we should heave to a bit ! ".   This I found very amusing, the thought of having two Captains, with the Captain's wife taking key decisions.

Xmas 1955 was celebrated at sea, and the catering staff made a big effort to create the Xmas spirit.   Being at sea, everyone was reasonably sober, and hilariously, the stewards decided to decorate the saloon for the event.   Someone had the bright idea to use condoms from the medical locker in place of balloons.   We all sat down to our festive meal surrounded by inflated and painted condoms with the little bobble on the end hanging gloomily around the bulkheads.

Whilst on this run, it happened that the crew decided to bring their girl friends along. They were mainly out of control in port when drink was freely available anyway, and so it happened that girls, and in one case, a man, took up residence in the cabins, and lived for weeks without detection. It was a big joke that we, the apprentices shared. Food was no problem, as the very efficient galley was situated centrally in the accommodation opposite the crew messroom. On the last trip up for phosphate however, catastrophe occurred. The orders were changed and we were directed to ports in New Zealand, where the ' passengers' were duly discovered, causing a huge rumpus. About the same time, when we were discharging in the North Island port of New Plymouth, my cabin mate, one of the other apprentices, decided to leave the ship and end his short career and stay with his Maori sweet heart that he had met . She claimed to be a Maori Princess. He planned his departure at night, and duly bequeathed his radio and a few other possessions to me, in exchange for my vow of silence for 24 hours, something which caused me considerable grief and criticism when his departure became known. It was quite rare for apprentices to ' run' to use the old Royal Navy expression, although many left the company before completing their apprenticeship when it became clear that such a life was not for them. I never saw, or heard from him again, although much later I heard that his parents had flown to New Zealand

to bring him back to Geordie land where he came from. Each port on these coasts brought their own events, but rarely went smoothly. It was mayhem, with a minor crisis each time we wanted to move on. There was no shortage of jobs for fit and willing men. This period in the 50's was perhaps the peak of the dockers or wharfies power, and their highly lucrative jobs were guarded jealously. This period was near to the peak of docker power in Europe and Australasia and their constant strikes akin to blackmail was one of the reasons attributed to the drive to containerisation by ship owners. As a result of the very tight closed shop mentality in Australian ports, there were a few occasions when gangs working at the hatches were short handed due to illness or holidays. Rather than allow anyone to get a position on the wharf, even temporarily, it was the practice to appeal to the ship to supply workers - the advantage being that when the ship sailed the vacancies were preserved, and no one had crept into the gang by the backdoor. By this means we came to earn riches beyond our wildest dreams! In my case, I was earning £4.11.8 per month as an apprentice on indentures, (plus keep, of course). but when we did a days work on the quay in Australia, we received wads of cash notes at the end of the day equivalent to several month's wages! Unbelievable. In addition, the working practices included ' awards' which were decided by the shop steward on the shift. This key member of the shore gangs wandered up and down the quay, settling the constant disputes, and judging if a particular issue deserved extra pay. To us, they were often laughable, but they were taken very seriously by our new work mates. There was ' stoop money' for having to bend down, dirt money, for handling boxes of carbon black from the USA, smell money, etc, and it all totted up to a sizeable sum. It was fun and the mood was very light hearted. We had a ball, but these instances of being ' seagulls' as the temporary wharfies were called, were all too few.

Eventually we loaded grain in bulk in the Spencer Gulf ports of Port Pirie, Port Lincoln, Wallaroo, and set off for Calcutta and Indian ports, where large grain shipments, mainly from the USA were helping to relieve the shortages at that time. While we were in the Spencer Gulf, one of the apprentices and myself, aided by the Maltese carpenter we had on board, built a sailing dinghy. We sewed the sails from duck canvas and we used the little boat whenever it looked feasible, slinging it overside with the derricks. It eventually came to grief, when we had to be towed back from a trip that went badly wrong. These ports also saw the worst excesses of the drunken crew, and little normal working took place.   There was difficulty keeping discipline and order mainly due to the ready access to dockside pubs. As mentioned, any shortfall in numbers however would be made up prior to sailing.

After discharging the grain in Indian ports, we were ordered to load gunnies in Calcutta for South America   Arriving in the Hooghly, my old stamping ground on the Inchanga, we tied up to buoys, and it happened that for a brief period we were double moored with another of the company's ships. Looking down on the deck of the other ship, and the Indian crew, our comedians from Liverpool were making some disparaging remarks, and I heard them say, " Look at those savages, not like us white savages! "

I can't think of anyone who welcomed their time at this port with it's abject poverty and teeming people, although the access up the river Hooghly was always an experience, and for me at least, the smell of smoke from the fires, the sights, and the sounds of haunting music emanating from compounds adjoining the road, especially in the evening, will always remain in my memory.   In the river, taking our break on deck it was not uncommon to see many animal carcasses floating downstream, and we also saw occasional bloated bodies.   Birds, especially Hawks would swoop down and steal any food held carelessly on deck.

There were always regular Bank Line ships calling in Calcutta, and a resident Superintendent looked after their affairs. He had a somewhat elevated status, and his almost daily visit to the ships was regarded with some deference. When we were in the river, on buoys, which was the usual arrangement, a sampan was used with a fascinating spectacle from the deck, as the adept operator sculled against the often very strong tide. This is something quite hard to describe, but to reach a landing stage level with the gangway, it was necessary to scull with full force at 90 degrees into the flow, and allow the crabbing sideways movement to complete the distance, judging the angle and power to drop alongside. Neatly in most cases, although it sometimes happened that the judgement went wrong and it could have spectacular results, much to the amusement of the onlookers on deck.

Still on the Maplebank, but with some new faces replacing most of the crew we lost in Australia, we set sail for South America and first stop Buenos Aires.   This was to be probably my favourite port, a sentiment shared by legions of seafarers then and now.   B.A. as it is known, offered so many attractions, and can only be described as an exciting port.   At the time we called there on the Maplebank, Juan Peron was still in power, although he was to be deposed shortly afterwards.   Our stay was hilarious. BA at that time had a notorious area near the docks called ' The Arches'. These were nothing more than arched spaces which were used as all sorts of. bars, clubs, and eating places. Violence was always present, although in general, a trip along there was fun.   They were tailor-made for our lovely Liverpool lads and the new arrivals we had picked up in Australia. . Some of the goings on are best left out of this account, but there was a late night when we apprentices ventured to an upstairs bar where the music and dancing was in full swing.   It wasn't long before I noticed some people, including our crew members urinating in the corner of the room. I also noticed a damp patch from below when we later moved on.   Presumably, they were too drunk or lazy to seek out the toilets.   But not too far gone to stagger round the dance floor usually leaning on their partner. So it went on, night after night. The routine was to rest until around 11pm, and then proceed ashore for a nights fun. The steaks were, and still are famous, and beef de Lomo world famous, at least among seafarers, was the most popular fare, usually after a tankful of drink. Oh, the pleasures and capacity of youth!   The big wide and attractive main thoroughfare named Veinticinco de Mayo, after the date of independence, was home to an array of cafes and bars, nearly all with music and a bevy of girls.   It was a feature of BA that the important and imposing buildings were marred by bullet scars from various rebellions, which struck me as bizarre.   I made many friends on these forays, and one particular group that I had chummed up with, gave me a photo, not unlike todays ' selfie', and below they had written the following sentence. ". May all Englishmen be as my new friend is ".   When we were at war over the Falklands in 1982, I was to think about that lovely sentiment on the old photo. After a week or two of the leisurely discharge of our gunny and jute cargo , the lads were getting a bit frayed round the edges, and things started to go from bad to worse, ending with a shooting as they returned in the early hours one morning.   The shots echoed round the ship, and I joined the breathless crew in the mess room after hearing the commotion.   They were telling how the civil guards had taken shots at them for their rowdy behaviour, kicking over bins etc, and singing loudly, as they returned to the ship.   After our stay, first in Monte

Video, across the River Plate in Uruguay, and then in Buenos Aires, we sailed for Brazil. Our destination was an ore loading port called Vittoria.   The ore was dumped into the holds in no time it seemed, and then it was home, or rather Bremen in Germany for discharge where we were all paid off to travel home on the ferry. The overnight ferry journey was the last chance for the wilder ones from our deck crew to cause mayhem, and they didn't disappoint.   The only person on deck who had seen out the voyage and who resisted the temptation to desert was a man called Smith who joined as an EDH (Efficient Deck hand) but who had been promoted up, finishing the trip as Bosun. He received a bad discharge at the pay off, something which I thought was unfair on the part of the Master, given that he had stuck out the voyage and had always been there when needed.   Inevitably, he had been drawn in to some of the high jinks around the world, but the suspicion was that he was the only remaining original crew member and a sort of scapegoat upon which revenge could be meted out.   My final view of him was on the ferry home. He was carrying a bird in a cage, which turned out to be dead with it's feet in the air, when the covering cloth was removed!   A fitting end to an amazing life changing trip.

Ahead of me now was what looked like an insurmountable barrier, as I was out of my apprenticeship, and facing the examination for a second mate's certificate. Strangely, I had been encouraged and also given hope by the Chief Officer on the Maplebank. He would pace up and down, distilling wisdom while I stood at the wheel night after night, and I gradually realised I was expected to pass this hurdle and go on to better things.

My education in life had advanced considerably during this long voyage, and I had come through it slightly older and wiser, even if there was still a long way to travel.

Chapter 7....M.V. " Irisbank"

The next step was a huge one in that examinations loomed.   It was time to face the Board of Trade exam for second Mates.   It was also a time when many Cadets or Apprentices chose to try another company.   This could be for shorter voyages or simply curiosity, and advise from shipmates was not lacking!   A Bank Line ship appointment in the 1950's however offered a rare chance to sail the world, visiting almost every corner, and spending time in a a host of ports, including many out of the way places, and I was more than happy to pledge my allegiance to the company especially as they offered to pay during the study time. The period in my case was a good 3 months, during which time I travelled daily up and down from Stanmore to Aldgate. It was a tedious journey, by buses and tube, but the time could be usefully used, silently rehearsing the Rules of the Road which had be to learnt by heart.   My long suffering sister agreed to quiz me night after night, as I recited them.   She could probably have been a useful companion in a collision situation on the bridge. The thinking behind this practice was presumably that if they could be repeated then they could be applied - a dubious proposition to my way of thinking, especially as we all learned them utterly parrot fashion.

The actual trips on offer were always for the statutory 2 years, but some ships were kept more or less on shorter spells that worked out at approx six months as they loaded down to Australasia, and back with Copra.   A suspicion existed that those appointed to these so called ' Copra ships' had some sort of ' pull' or were favoured in some mysterious way.   Either way, what awaited you was pure unadulterated magic! This was a British shipping company, unlike any other. Similar to many, but head and shoulders above the pack.

52

After my success in obtaining a second mate's certificate, I was appointed to the
M.V. Irisbank.   She was a real old timer, built in 1930, and another war survivor,
with twin screws and a decent turn of speed at 14 knots when both engines were
working satisfactorily, which was not always the case.   I joined in dry dock, and
soon we were on our way again to the U.S. Gulf.   Conditions on this old ship were
very basic.   No fresh water was available, unless hand carried in from the pumps
on or below decks, but salt water was laid on.   A bath, normal enough looking, had
a steam pipe attached to the side, the idea being that water, either salt or fresh,
laboriously carried in, would be rapidly heated.   This copper steam pipe was
swivelled, and the business end was swung around and poked under the water
before the valve was opened.   It made a very loud raucous noise not unlike an
animal being strangled.   A health and safety inspectors bonanza, except there
weren't any around in those days. Adjacent to the sink was a handy copper tank
which could also be filled with fresh water for heating electrically.   Bizarrely, it
also served as a boiler for eggs in bad weather when the galley had to shut down.
The author devised a way of trapping a sock under the lid with the toe containing an
egg dangling in the boiling water. It worked a treat!

It soon became clear that the Master was a strict authoritarian of the old school.
He stayed aloof and critical, and it was difficult to please, but slowly I learned how
to keep out of trouble.   Looking back all these years later, I have a lot of respect
for that man's memory.   For one thing he had come through the war at sea,
something which we youngsters tended to overlook.   Also, he had qualities that I
cherish today like reliability and dependability.   He was a decent and trustworthy
Master who carried a medical problem stoically, and we must have tested him to the
limit.   At the time I was disappointed to be told that my place was on the wings of
the bridge, I.e.out in the open, unless I had a good reason to be inside.   This is
laughable by today's standards, but that is how it was. I could only stay in the
chartroom or wheelhouse if I was working sights, or needing to alter course, or
signal etc.   A pattern of watchkeeping evolved, the main plank of which was

position finding.   Other duties depended on the location, I.e. If there was land in sight, but lays there was the need to keep a sharp lookout for other vessels. Then, a regular duty for an officer of the watch was to ensure that the big open ventilators throughout the length of the ship were always off the wind I.e. It was not accepted that rain should enter and spoil any cargo below.   It was more important obviously with grain or sensitive cargoes, but they were never allowed to face into the wind, unless on the rare occasions when ventilation was required, when the lee vent of a pair would be swivelled around to face into the wind.   The laborious altering of these vents was always done by the stand-by quartermaster who would be summonsed with the blast of a whistle from the bridge.   Some nights this could be a painful regular occurrence as the wind shifted around.

Food in the Bank Line was usually satisfactory without any frills.   The saloon table would be attractively laid out, with often the menu stuck in the prongs of a fork!   Curry and rice featured strongly, and appeared occasionally on the breakfast menu.   The curry concoctions were a work of art, the author's favourite being one with a sea of shimmering oil with halves of hard boiled eggs floating freely.   The colour of the surface changed into different hues as it moved.   The apprentices on any ship were always hungry, but in extremis it was possible to cadge a chapatti from the Indian cooks or Bhandaries, who catered for the deck and engine room crew.   On the older Bank Line ships, a distinctive feature was steel accommodation blocks either abeam of the foremast or mainmast and on either side.   These housed the crew galley, and also toilet blocks.   Arriving in a port anywhere in the world, day or night, it was often possible to pick out the outline of one of the old Bank Line stalwarts - true work horses of the oceans they were. Apart from the distinctive blocks on deck, the early ships from the 1920's and 30's had derricks which were usually lattice type, a box with criss cross strengthening on all four sides.   The steam winches would all be clattering away as the cargo was furiously loaded or discharged, with a string of barges alongside.   Decks were sheathed in pine, and scrubbed up or holystoned after a long port stay, they turned near white and glistened in the wet.   Open rails instead of today's bulwarks complete the picture.

Watches on the bridge followed a strict routine, and this was long before Satellite and Global positioning spoiled the fun, and agony, of position finding.   The actual wheelhouse on the old timers was quite often small but somehow homily, if that is possible. Before automatic steering, a quartermaster stood silently behind the wheel, and he was watching a magnetic compass in the binnacle, steering a course marked up on a chalk board by the officer of the watch. There would be a manual voice pipe to the Master's cabin, a brass telegraph, and a small side table with a dim or coloured bulb. During this period, the first radar sets were being fitted and space was found for the display unit on a low table.   Early models were unreliable and became the bane of Sparkie's lives as they were hauled out regularly to fix breakdowns.   Many Masters ordered their use very reluctantly, or reserved the time they were switched on to pilotage areas, or passing the many islands in the Pacific and elsewhere.   Approaching the Mississippi SW pass entrance on this trip, the pilot asked for the radar to be switched on, only to be told by the Master that we didn't use it except when necessary.   The pilot replied, " Mister, if that radar is not switched on now, we are going straight to anchor". The radar went on.

The doors either side of the wheelhouse led out to a short bridge wing with 'cabs' for weather protection at the ship's side. These heavy doors slid open and shut and were held in place with wooden wedges. Getting them right was a special skill. The bridge front had drop down wooden dodgers in the traditional manner, but one or two shorter Masters were known to use a box to see forward.

Above the wheelhouse, the so called ' monkey island' was accessed by short vertical ladders, and on a raised platform would be the standard compass with an azimuth ring on top, protected by a binnacle hood.   In those far off days, this compass was a crucial part of the navigation, and was in constant use for bearings, both of heavenly bodies, and for coastal bearings as the ship progressed. This exposed area was also a haven of peace and quiet, and could be a magical place at night with a huge canopy of stars and planets, especially in mid Pacific in clear weather when the sight was often breathtaking. All of the radio stations from the USA West coast would come flooding in on certain nights, creating an odd feeling as we were days from land.

Bank Line ships also carried a huge range of charts as standard, running into thousands. These were stowed below the chartroom table behind the wheelhouse, and correcting them could be a nightmare. The trick was to keep up to date, otherwise the task became hopeless. Because of the range of charts, it was standard practice to pull out and correct only those charts needed for the immediate voyage ahead. Correction of existing Admiralty charts, and supplementary charts could be obtained in major ports like Sydney or London, but more often than not, the second mate, whose responsibility it was, would have to somehow prepare the courses, and ensure the charts were up to date. The ship regularly received the well known ' Notices to Mariners' for this purpose. On this trip, there was an occasion rounding the coast near Cape Town when a new light suddenly appeared, and which had been overlooked from the corrections. Our strict Master was less than pleased. On the bulkhead would be an impressive array of Admiralty sailing directions in a rack or two. Inside these volumes was a cornucopia of fascinating information, some of it handed down and still printed from Captain Cook's time. Many a boring watch was saved by delving into these books which seemed to be a mixture of old and new, probably stemming from the fact that there is a long British maritime history garnered worldwide, and alterations and additions seemed to be added ad hoc. In the chartroom would be a settee, often with boxed sextants resting on it, and the standard chart table with a shaded lamp. At night a tray of sandwiches and tea making equipment appeared. Cockroaches abounded. So much so they often took on pet status as they appreciated the sandwiches more than we did.

This ballast leg heading for the U.S. Gulf, was a necessary part of positioning the ships, and I for one, was oblivious until much later in management ashore, how much this non paying leg cost the company.   It was a reflection of the tight conference arrangements between shipping companies how difficult it was to pick up a cargo on someone else's patch.   We had the Gulf ports to look forward to however, and the usual hectic programme of loading.   The Superintendents ashore, who governed the loading pattern, were inclined to sail the ship at nights and to use these hours for positioning the ship in the morning just along the coast. This meant of course that sleep was a problem and usually taken in catnaps.   We wended our way through the oil platforms that dot the Gulf of Mexico, and started the loading of Potash in the lower holds.   In Galveston, one of my favourite ports, we spent some time cruising the bars and stocking up on denim and to my eyes, beautiful cotton shirts and shorts for the tropics. At that time, the main street was very much like those in the cowboy movies, complete with hitching rails, and swing doors.   It was amusing and a bit sad some 30 years later when I returned on business, seeking out the haunts for old times sake. Wandering towards my old stamping ground, I discovered that the main street had been ' Disneyfied' , to coin a phrase.   It was preserved for tourists, complete with signs, and enhanced features reminiscent of Hollywood westerns.

Loading went smoothly, and we topped off in the crescent city of New Orleans.

After the canal transit which went smoothly, the long Pacific crossing from Balboa to Auckland in New Zealand gave me a chance to   improve my standing with the Master, but it was hard work. Nothing seemed to please.   I was sustained by the second mate, who had become a friend, and who was a rebel in his own right.   We stood together on the bridge for the noon day sights, and when the Master joined us there was always a reverent silence. Anything else was frowned upon. We often got our revenge by ganging up on him when the time came to compare positions, something he must have been aware of. Two against one made him tut tut, and concede that his calculations might not be accurate.

There was a hilarious moment one day when we were standing silently in a line. Probably from boredom, I had hit upon the idea of having an alternative life, and the one I chose, completely in my imagination, was a cycle tour around Britain. The second mate and myself usually swapped notes about our respective activities around this time at noon. There was the usual wait for the sun to reach its noon zenith, and he asked me quietly. " Where have you cycled to today, then? ". After a pause, I said " I haven't got anywhere, I had a puncture! ". This cracked us both up, and earned us some stern looks from the Captain. Anyone familiar with astronomical sights will know that it is more an art than a science, so often although we were confident in our results, we were probably all wrong! This is long before satellite navigation arrived. What a boon that would have been, but some of the fun inevitably disappeared.

A strange event also occurred one night in mid Pacific when I was on the evening watch from 8 to 12, and we were passing one of the many so called uninhabited islands. It was dark, and we were steaming along at the usual 5 miles distant from this small unlit island near the Galapagos islands. Pacing up and down the bridge wing I saw a small white light ashore, and it was clearly blinking SOS. I waited and yes, there it was again. I called the Captain up to the bridge and he stood silently looking. Nothing happened for a while, but then the light resumed and he grudgingly acknowledged to me he had seen it, and disappeared into the chartroom to study the sailing directions for that area. We sailed on, and his comments were. " Oh, well, there is a trading schooner that calls here every six months". Readers might feel critical of this non action, but I have asked myself many times what I might have done in his shoes. No doubt he was weighing up the delay and displeasure in Head Office, coupled with the fact that we only had cumbersome heavy wooden lifeboats to pass through any surf around the place. We didn't have a large scale chart, if there was one, of such a small island. Nothing could have been attempted until daylight anyway, which meant drifting or steaming up and down until daybreak. It was a difficult call, but I still had that niggling feeling we should have responded.

Soon we passed through the twin islands of Bora Bora. in the Society islands, not far from Tahiti. First the peaks lifted out of the ocean, then the water shallowed and turned light blue as we progressed. Pleasure craft were sailing off the shore. It doesn't sound very exciting, but when there were weeks of nothing but empty ocean all around, any change of scenery is welcome. We had one of the old wet paper echo sounders in the chartroom, which worked quite well providing the paper was fresh and wet. Usually this meant straight out of the wrapper, as it dried out very quickly. Spare rolls were kept handy in sealed packets, but should the paper dry out, results rapidly faded. It worked by marking the paper with a rotating stylus making a clickety clack noise as it rotated. It was straight out of the ark by today's standards, but it was a major step up from the old Kelvin deep sea sounding wire which was still in use on some ships. In those days we also trailed a log astern on a special line, and this rotated and recorded a reading which approximated to the distance travelled. Once a watch, the seacunny or quartermaster below would read the mileage and report it to the bridge. The business end of the log line was a copper or brass tool shaped like a mini rocket and sporting curved fins which made it rotate through the water. These were occasionally bitten off by fish. They could also pick up debris on rare occasions. When the log was replaced, the old one was sometimes adapted into an ornament by some imaginative person. My friend from that trip still has a polished version which he turned into an attractive table lamp.

After a few weeks on this transit of the Pacific, we finally approached the pilot station off Moreton island which serves the Queensland port of Brisbane. It had taken us the best part of four weeks. The weather was too rough for the pilot to board and we waited while they signalled furiously with an extremely bright light and which I found very difficult to read due to it being so close and strong. In exasperation, the Master sent below for my pal, the second mate, who was roused from his sleep! Ignominy! The signals whizz kid from sea school had struggled and failed to read a signal in time of need. It just added to my feeling of inadequacy which was being relayed to me on an almost daily basis.

We worked our way round the coast, discharging the usual mix of tractors, general cargo, including lamp black, hickory handles, drummed oil and additives, and assorted pallets, together with the bulk cargo. This had to be discharged using shoreside grabs, but on the ships gear. It was common for the sulphur dust to sometimes ignite on these occasions. Sparks from metal brushing on metal often triggered blue flashes which could be spectacular. And once again there were opportunities to work alongside the wharfies to earn extra cash. Bill Haley and the Comets were at their peak at this time, with ' Rock around the clock' and other hits and we were to see him on trips ashore as he toured the cities in New Zealand and Australia. My memory is of crowded dance halls, an electric atmosphere with the loud beat, and a haze of blue smoke bobbing up and down in unison with the dancers. There were nasty scenes reported as the seats and fittings were flung around by over hysterical and drunken revellers. Little did we realise we were viewing an iconic band!

Life on board was good, and there was a camaraderie between the deck and engine room officers, and not forgetting the Sparkie, or radio officer seconded from the Marconi company. He was a wild card with very independent ideas and a challenging streak which made life interesting, given the stern Master we were under. There were various moments of rebellion - coloured hair, mohican hair cut, and raucous trumpet playing around the ship, all received with equanimity, partly due, I suspect, to the fact that Sparkie was a Marconi employee at the end of the day, and slightly insulated from normal discipline.   He was also a strong trad jazz fan and I recall him arranging tickets to see Louise Armstrong on stage in Sydney. We also celebrated my 21st birthday in port, which at least allowed us to have some celebratory drinks, away from the rather muted atmosphere on board. Watches on the bridge followed a strict routine, and this was long before Satellite and Global positioning spoiled the fun of position finding.   The actual wheelhouse on the old timers was quite often small but somehow homily,   During this period, the first radar sets were being fitted and space was found for the display unit on a low table.   Early models were unreliable and became the bane of Sparkie's lives as they were hauled out regularly to fix breakdowns.   Many Masters ordered their use very reluctantly, or reserved the time they were switched on to pilotage areas, or passing the many islands in the Pacific and elsewhere.   The doors either side of the wheelhouse led out to a short bridge wing with 'cabs' for weather protection at the ship's side.

Orders came that we were to take a full cargo of grain for India, and to sail around to Fremantle in Western Australia to load.   Someone back in Head Office decided in their wisdom that they could save money by getting the ships staff to erect the necessary shifting boards. These were a requirement with bulk grain cargoes. This work, normally carried out by shipwrights, involved erecting large wooden partitions to prevent grain from shifting in adverse weather, particularly when heavy rolling. Hence the name.   A diagram was produced from somewhere, and the officers and apprentices, aided by the Chinese carpenter spent several days swinging around the holds precariously at sea, finally producing a credible version of the drawings. It was the first time I had done any manual work since signing on in the elevated status of third mate, and I enjoyed the change.   Arriving in Fremantle though, all hell broke loose.   The wharfies who were in cahoots with the shipwrights and in particular their union, took a very dim view of us robbing them of what was their work, and they swiftly condemned our efforts. For good measure, they engineered a detailed survey of our wooden boats, and I remember watching the surveyor going to work on the planking with a pointed tool, finally, triumphantly, springing the planking away from the stem bar.   The boat was condemned and as there was no replacement available in Australia we were stuck in Fremantle on a lay up berth until a replacement could be shipped in.   The long sandy beach was only 100 yds away across the road, and we spent several more or less idyllic weeks there, swimming, and playing cricket etc in the day, and visiting the bars at night. It was tough.   Once again, in later years I came to think about the loss to the company, but any sympathy was tempered by the knowledge that the shifting board fiasco ordered by them had been the cause .

We sailed to India.   First port was Visagapatam where I had the satisfaction of leaning over the bridge front after we rang ' Finished with engines ' to see the hold below opened up and the bulk grain filling the space, right up to the top of the coamings. An amazing sight was the swarm of dock workers who set to.   As it was bulk grain, the technique was to bag it there and then, before making up sling loads for swinging ashore. A man with a scoop stood with his back to the open bag held by another, his legs apart, and then frantically scooped away until each bag was quickly filled.   Another worker stood ready with needle and thread and quickly secured the top of each bag as it filled.   The swarm of ants analogy came to mind watching this, but it was efficient in a labour intensive way.   It sounds a bit mawkish now, but rightly or wrongly, I did feel a sense of pride coupled with satisfaction that we had successfully steered this cargo into their hands, all the way from Australia.

This trip dragged on.   In many ways it was a sort of catharsis for me, clearing my head with all those long hours walking up and down the bridge wings, on those interminable watches.   Looking back now, it was a struggle with myself, accepting my place, deciding on goals, and dealing with immediate challenges like the ever censoring Master that I was contracted to, and from whom I could not easily escape.   In Visag, as the port is known, I worked the night shifts, while the piles of grain slowly lowered in the holds.   They were long sultry nights with nothing to do except watch out for rain, eat the curly sandwiches from the night tray put out by stewards, and administer first aid to the spasmodic injuries that the dock workers had.   I sat on the iron bitts on the deck, and read a copy of Time magazine from cover to cover. Some of the injuries were serious, and I had the sad job of comforting a dying man on one occasion. He looked alright, but he had been crushed in the head by a sling of cargo, sandwiching him against the steel hatch coaming. His head had literally lifted where a thin trickle of blood ran around the crack.   Following the Medical guide kept on board I could only treat him for shock - warm sweet tea is prescribed, and it was his last as he died a few minutes later. We sat on the deck, surrounded by his fellow workers, and with me fussing over him, but nothing could be done to save him.   There was another occasion when a man in the hold had to be lifted out on a stretcher and he slipped down and nearly out of the stretcher as he was being lifted in the air.   It was the wrap around type, designed for lifting from one end, but something went dramatically wrong and he was left half way out before he very fortunately jammed tight, to the relief of everyone watching.

About this time, I began to realise how nice the unsophisticated people around the world are.   It had surprised me in Trinidad, talking to the workers in the hold, and now in India, I had many engaging conversations with ordinary fun loving people, and looking back over the years, I would say as a broad generalisation, that the poorer and more primitive people are, the more sincere and genuine they are. There is a simple charm and openness that often has been lost by folk in more so called advanced countries.   Do we learn all the wrong things as we grow up?

We trundled on around the world on our first circuit, but this trip was to be later marked by some events that would test me and my shipmates.   After a return visit to my old haunts in Calcutta, we loaded the usual jute and gunnies for ports all around Africa, East, South, and West.   I had missed out on one of my cherished ambitions when we commenced loading whilst in the Hooghly river for the West coast of South America, and some 17 ports in Chile, Peru, and Ecuador. This route includes a passage through the Magellan Straits, something I dearly wanted to do, but it wasn't to be, because without warning the orders were changed, and the cargo we had just loaded was removed!   So off we went to Africa.

There was a sordid or funny occasion in one of the West African ports, according to your point of view, when a willing girl was ferried out to us at anchor, and passed around all night.   Even worse, she had been placed on a chair in the centre of a room, and surrounded by hairy blokes deciding what ever they decided! Something then went wrong, because she called the police in the morning and we were all paraded on the boat deck for identification and retribution.   The girl passed slowly along the line, pointing out various individuals, but again something was amiss, because she managed to pick out both guilty and innocent men! Eventually though, money was produced and paid over, and she went off more or less contented, riding ashore on the police boat.

We continued along the coast, calling at all the ports, sometimes only to discharge a few tons.   Most of the ports were served from an anchorage, and so called kru boats, big and seaworthy, skilfully handled, took our cargo ashore.   In Freetown, I had occasion to go ashore with some pals, and I was bowled over by the beauty of all the young topless girls walking unconsciously along often with baskets perched on their head.

The difference in the style and layout of the port cities was very noticeable too, the French towns being the smartest by far in my opinion.   Dakar in Senegal being a perfect example. Neat squares with palms, and boulevards as in Metropolitan

France.   Ditto, Abidjan in the Ivory Coast.   For some reason I always felt that Africans speaking fluent French was a bit incongruous.

Once discharge was finally completed, it was across the Atlantic again this time loading bitumen back in Trinidad, bound for New Zealand.   My stevedore friend was still in the gangs, and still ruing his lot in life.   Even at my young age, I understood his dilemma .   I hope he made a break and achieved his ambitions.

We discharged all around the New Zealand coast, ending up in the very southern port of Bluff, famous for oysters.   They were not my taste, but they were immensely popular with the ships officers, washed down of course with suitable quantities of beer.   Leaving Bluff to load in Australia, we rounded Stewart Island at the southern end of New Zealand.   We then lost a man overboard.   The sea was rough - and cold - and he was engaged in helping to dump slings of dunnage wood over the side, a common practice then.   The rails had been removed and a full sling gently nudged him over the side as the ship rolled slowly. It must have been a slow motion nightmare for him.   The next 4 hours were spent looking over the ocean which had angry whitecaps and a heavy swell running. The sea was inhospitable that afternoon.   I chose to climb the mainmast with binoculars to better scan the horizon, and I sat uncomfortably for a long time cramped up and gripping the round truck for safety, but without spotting anything. To make matters worse, the Captain for some reason was reversing the engines occasionally, presumably because they had spotted something from the bridge, and this vibrated the top mast violently, whipping it backwards and forwards. I was like the fly on the end of a swatter, but managed to cling on, scared as hell.   As it got dark it was decided to resume our course, and then just when the search had been called off, and I returned to the bridge, we all spotted flocks of sea birds feeding on something in the water.   It was our shipmate. One of our clumsy wooden lifeboats, the motorboat, was prepared and several of us volunteered to go.   It's the sort of thing you do when young and without a thought. After some difficulty with an engine room discharge flooding the boat as it was lowered, we set off in quite heavy weather, my pal Jimmy the second mate at the helm. He did a great job, skilfully preventing the boat from flooding or broaching - not an easy task. We had rushed to get in the boat, and the rather perilous situation dawned on me as we cast off   It was my first experience of a smallish boat in the open ocean, and the Irisbank disappeared completely when we were in the troughs of the waves. I started singing my head off, later attributed to nerves by folk who know about these situations.   When we got to the body, it was relatively easy to roll the poor young seaman straight into the boat, aided by the fact that we were low in the water from being partially swamped.   First we had to use oars to beat off the insistent birds feeding on his face.   They had pecked out his cheeks. I helped roll his body onto the thwart, and was shocked to see the condition with all the teeth exposed, and even eyes hanging out.   On return to the ship, things got worse.   The ship was rolling heavily, and although we managed to engage the lifting hooks, we swung wildly out and then crashed back hitting the hull , severely damaging our planking. The body came close to shooting out of the boat, but worse than that I had trapped my fingers badly in the lifting block when hooking on, and as a result of the lifting and crashing around.   I must have been screaming, because someone with an axe started to swing at the rope falls to release my hand, when suddenly it was freed by the action of a passing wave, lifting the boat high and causing the ropes to slacken.   Out came my crushed fingers, and we continued up the ship's side, relieved to be free of the turmoil.   Once up in the davits I was shocked to see the boat side completely stove in, and the copper buoyancy tanks, hanging out. These are normally stowed along the sides below the side thwarts.   The boat later needed replacement - our second one on this trip.

Glad to be safely back, we then got orders to apply artificial respiration to the poor seaman! It was long past the stage where any chance of life remained, but orders are orders.   Eventually our Asian crew prepared the body for a burial at sea, which they were to carry out. This also turned out to be a sad fiasco, as the plan was to lower the body, now in a canvas shroud, down the ships side on staging with attendant seamen either end. Due to the adverse weather, the staging got halfway down when a huge wave swept along the side of the ship and the body disappeared into the wake . As it was now dark, we resumed the voyage, leaving matters to fortune.   The canvas shroud was weighted, so would have found a resting place at the bottom of the ocean. A really sad affair, and we later packed up his belongings for return to relatives in Calcutta.   A lifebelt washed up on the shore of South Island much later in the year, and the finders, curious, contacted the owners back in London.

Arriving in Australia, we had the good fortune to be in Melbourne for the November 1956 Olympics, and in our usual cheeky way, managed to gain entry for a day without paying.   Also in port was the royal yacht, Britannia, and some of us wandered along the quay to admire the glossy blue hull and beautiful white superstructure. She was a handsome ship with a classic profile. I was to see her again in different locations before she and I both went into retirement.

About this time there was a terrible drunken fight which unfortunately took place mostly in my small cabin.   We had signed on a particularly aggressive Australian engineer, who normally was a pleasant enough individual, but when with drink, he became extremely unpleasant and suspicious of everyone.   A huge fracas broke out one evening while we were tied up in Melbourne.   The mate ended up in an ambulance on the way to hospital, and the trouble maker continued around the decks on the rampage like a wild bull.   By this time, his head was running blood from where bottles had been smashed over him, and he was still going strong.   Our Scottish engineers were no slouches in a fight, I realised, but I was not in their league. Eventually, the police were called and stalked him round the deck rather like the wild animal he was, before they quickly subdued him and whizzed him down the gangway. This was not before he had attacked the poor Indian seacunny or quartermaster,   manning the gangway.   It was a grim episode. In the middle of this, I decided I had had enough, and fled ashore, spending a chilly night in a bus shelter a mile or two away! My motto was. "He who fights and runs away, lives to fight another day". and it seemed to work, because when I returned in the early hours, things seemed normal. I gingerly stepped into the accommodation expecting the worst, but all was quiet. My white cabin walls however, had blood stains all over them, and the cabin deck was covered in broken glass which crunched underfoot. For me, I felt this was the end. I started packing my things without any clear idea where to go. It is in these situations that the Seaman's Mission comes into it's own, and would probably have been my temporary home. However, midway through packing, my nemesis appeared at the door enquiring politely what I was doing. It was the Captain, who had been conspicuously absent the previous evening. Maybe his dicky heart had influenced his decision to stay above the fracas, both literally and figuratively, because he would have heard the rumpus only a few feet up the stairway to his cabin. Whatever the reason, this was out of character, and it was the first time I had seen him on the back foot. ". I'm leaving". I said. " I've had enough". There was a pause, and then he said. " You don't have to go". ". I will take care of it" meaning our troublesome engineer, and this he did. We never saw him again, and I unpacked and sailed on.

We rarely saw this Master relax or let down his guard, but there were some occasions on my evening watch when he would wander up to the bridge, and in the right mood would come out the bridge wing where I was pacing as per his instructions, and we would lean on the dodger looking forward side by side. No eye contact was made, but he would open up a little in the dark night, telling me about his worries, mainly his health. He had a fear that he might die on the operating table, and years later, long after we had all left this ship, I heard second hand that exactly this had happened and his premonition had come true. We had parted at the end of the voyage when we all flew home from Africa, and he made the trip on an Elder Dempster passenger ship due to heart problems.

During the endless watches at sea, there was one issue which dogged me, and that was the necessity to please this Master with an error observation, duly entered into the error book, and better still one which conformed to his expectations. He came to the bridge each watch like clockwork, and made a beeline for this little book, studying the entries. I should explain to non shipping readers that back in the days covered by this chapter, the course steered, and the navigation was dependent on the accuracy of a magnetic compass. This compass, a beautiful instrument which was a card pivoted on a needle and floating in a dampening liquid, was affected by the two outside forces of variation, which depended on the area or location the ship was in, and was marked on the chart, and by deviation. Deviation alters with the actual direction of the ships head, and is caused by the influence of iron in the vicinity of the compass The combined effect is known as the compass error, and this could be fairly accurately calculated by taking a bearing of a prominent star, which of course requires a clear sky or opening through which the bearing could be taken. The absence of an entry in the book required explaining. An unusual entry was worse, and definitely suspect, even if correct. Obviously, there was a temptation to cheat and enjoy an easy life, but I am pleased to say I never succumbed. There was absolutely no relaxing on the 8 to 12 watch until this important ritual had been completed AND approved.

On we went, and after loading jute bales again in Chittagong and ports in the Sundarbans , one of the largest Mangrove forests in the world, it was off to African ports. When we had arrived off Chittagong harbour on the Karnaphuli river we had struck a sand bank during my watch. The action appeared to me to be in slow motion but we were at full speed on a clear day around noon. Looking ahead, the water suddenly appeared to be rippling ahead in a strange way. Alarmed, I had switched on the old paper sounder which clacked away as the stylus whizzed round and round. While I watched mesmerised almost, the line marking the bottom of the sea came up steeply towards us, and I rushed back into the wheelhouse, just in

time to witness us thumping the bank beneath the waves. We heeled right over, and a wave created by the collision swept up and over the boat deck, with water swishing down to the engine room via the skylights which were open. This triggered a frantic call from the engineers asking what the hell is going on! In the meantime, I had rung down to stop the engines and sheered off to port, calling the Master to the bridge.

Protest was noted when we berthed, (a technical procedure) and it later transpired to my relief that the buoy supposedly marking the shoal had been dragged away by a recent hurricane to a false position. No serious damage had been done, but we were not to know this until dry-docking later in the voyage.

A young elephant was loaded, or rather walked on deck, for transport to a zoo near Durban. The poop was piled high with young banana trees, the hearts of which he relished, tearing the centre out with his powerful trunk. It was to be his sole source of food for several weeks. He drank buckets of water carried to him by the apprentices. They were charged with his care and watering , and the elephant was chained on deck near the main mast. So far, so good, but it was to end in tragedy. Whatever the reason, he slowly got poorly, and eventually died within sight of his release in Durban. It was sad and ironic that he had weathered so many weeks, but succumbed within sight of release. His stay had been near six weeks, and he had amused us greatly, flattening buckets with his front feet, and balancing precariously on the rails by sitting on them so they bent under his weight. Opinions

The young elephant walking onboard in India, watched by the Captain in a Topee.

..and being dropped over the side dead, and within sight of Durban.

varied about the cause of his death, but no one really knew.   I favoured the broken heart theory, and secretly felt I knew what it meant.   His body was ignominiously hoisted up by the derricks and dropped into the sea off Durban for the sharks.

This voyage was near an end.   We learned that we would be flown home from Bathurst in West Africa, and when the day arrived we boarded a Viking type aircraft for the flight home to Blackbush airport.   The replacement crew had flown out on the same chartered plane, but we were destined not to meet, as we passed to and fro the airport. The runway was military style, with metal mesh sheets laid on the grass, and it was my first flight.   On board the Viking type aircraft, there was a huge beam running across the cabin, a strange feature on this model.   I soon noticed sweating hands after take off, which the stewardesses explained were the result of nerves. The pilots chose to buzz the ship after take off and we swooped down in a stomach churning dive, which didn't help things much. We then set off to follow the African coast northwards.   I did notice the pilots up front looking ahead through binoculars when the cockpit door was open. In those days this journey had to be broken halfway and we all spent a glorious night in the Rock Hotel in Gibraltar,   wallowing in hot water baths, and enjoying the delights of the dining room. There was a further refuelling stop at Biarritz in France in the morning, and then we arrived safely at Blackbush as night was falling. All the lights were twinkling on approach and as the coach swept us up to London we passed all the picturesque pubs with fairy lights and welcoming forecourts. It was pure magic to my mind, and the contrast from our previous two years of primitive living could not be greater.   I was a bit overwhelmed emotionally, but already wistful for my old life on board!

Appendix 1.   The Company history from 1885

The apprenticeship as a deck apprentice in the Bank Line was merely one of many on offer in the maritime world after the war. British shipping companies, although reeling from the damaging and tragic effect of world war 2, were re tonnaging. There was a large number of Lines serving every corner of the world, and some tramping companies roamed the globe between the limits of the arctic and antarctic. The Bank Line was one of the finest examples of this seagoing gypsy world. They also had a network of liner routes served by a rotating stream of company ships.   For those familiar with the Merchant Navy at that time, there was a subtle but distinctive choice of employment, and an unwritten but real perception of status.   The perception was not always accurate, but a sort of maritime snobbery existed whereby companies were judged by their appeal to those lucky mariners eyeing up a future career. At the higher end of the desirable companies can be listed P & O, Cunard etc, and at the bottom end there were many tramping companies that had acquired a poor reputation - either for food, conditions, discipline, or more often for carrying out very long voyages.   The perception was just that.   The reality often was different, and most companies had their loyal officers and crew.

The Bank Line is the story of a remarkable achievement. How one man built an amazing shipping empire throughout his long life, weathering the ups and downs along the way, and going from strength to strength. This man was born Andrew

Weir, later to be Lord Inverforth. From 1885 onwards for well over 100 years, this iconic shipping company criss crossed the globe with a fleet of up to 50 ships. Trading to all ports in the world within 60 degrees north and south, and visiting remote locations on all the continents, the ships could regularly be seen in most ports with their distinctive buff and black funnel.   For this writer, sailing on the long and often mysterious voyages in the 1950's, the sight of another Bank Line

ship toiling away in an arrival port engendered a feeling hard to describe. It was a strange mixture of pride, curiosity and camaraderie. Today, the ships are all gone, another victim, mainly of rampant containerisation, but it might be said that the special hunger for success died with the founder. It was a magic ingredient only gifted to true entrepreneurs,

Grain Trader, " Olivebank" as she was known in 1936. Seen leaving Sydney for Falmouth (for orders). Part of the Gustav Erikson fleet.

The build up began in sail, continued into steam, and then continued into a fleet of modern diesel vessels. Like many of the traditional shipping companies, the fleet successfully weathered two world wars, and numerous economic crises, including the Great Depression.   A heavy price was paid however. For example, a venture into tankers in the Second World War, owning ships with names beginning with an ' Inver' prefix ended remarkably with the whole fleet of seven vessels being lost to torpedoes and mines from enemy action.

The full story of the Bank Line growth would fill a fascinating book or two, but this brief overview of the 'glory' years from a mariner's perspective, only aims to highlight the scale of the growth, together with some of the achievements and some of the setbacks.

The entrepreneurial owner mentioned

above was born into a family of cork merchants in Scotland, and he was imbued with the essential ingredients for success - hard work, shrewdness, and above all, vision. The sailing fleet he built up rapidly became the largest under the red ensign.

Today, we have not only the benefit of hindsight, but a clearer picture of this sailing ship achievement, and it is impossible not to be awed by the risk that owners, and particularly seafarers faced in that age. Nearly half of the vessels met an untimely end from stranding, burning, or simply going missing on passage, an all too frequent ending. One noted graveyard in the sailing ship era was the trade with coal from Australian ports like Newcastle to the Nitrate loading berths in Chile. Looking looking through the fleet lists, this was the fate of at least 3 of the Weir fleet. Of all the handsome sailing ships built for Andrew Weir, the Beechbank, one of an 8 ship order, stands out for she somehow managed 32 years afloat, a rare feat. Wrecks from the fleet dotted the world, for example at Goto Island, Japan (Ann Main), Goodwin sands,(Hazelbank),Isle of Arran, (Elmbank), Mozambique Channel,(Fernbank), Iquique Chile,(Oakbank), Recife,(Trafalgar), Chinchas,Chile, (Forthbank),Scilly Isles, (Thornliebank), and many more. Numbers of vessels were sold out of the fleet to Norwegian owners over the years, no doubt when good money was to be made. Then, only 11 short years after starting up, and already with a substantial fleet of sailing vessels, Andrew Weir took delivery of his first steam driven ship, the Duneric in 1896, a measure of the confidence and ambition that drove him forward. Before leaving the sailing ships, mention should be made of probably the most famous of them, the Olivebank. This beautiful vessel made fast passages, for example taking only 85 days from Melbourne to Falmouth in 1900. She achieved passages which were up there with the best of her class, and Sea

Breezes magazine of 1935 reports in the 'Signal Station' section of that time, Olivebank, arr. Port Lincoln, 19th January, 85 days from Elsinore. This put her firmly in the same class as the renowned Pamir and Passat and the other. ' Flying P Liners' of the F Laeisz fleet. Olivebank was sold to Norwegian owners in 1913, and in 1924 became a part of the well known Gustav Erikson fleet of Finland in whose hands she continued to make fast passages, mainly in the Australian grain trade. In the early 30's she was regularly featuring alongside the flying 'P's' and others competing on the long passage from Europe to mainly the Spencer Gulf in south Australia and back. A typical decent passage was around 85 to 100 days to Falmouth, i.e. A good 3 month voyage each way. These hazardous passages were faithfully reported in the magazine " Sea Breezes". In 1939, Olivebank met her end when she was mined in the North Sea. A few fortunate survivors were rescued from a mast which remained sticking up above the waves.

One of the talents of Andrew Weir was a gift for creating a strong network of worldwide agents, many of whom were also friends and business partners, and who shared independent trading and shipping activities in their own sphere. These bonds grew very strong, and they were to form the sinews of world wide shipping services that endured for decades. Over the years patterns emerged, and Lines were created with fixed schedules, the loading not always carried out by the same ships, but by one of the company vessels that could be stemmed on to the loading ports just at the right time. The uninitiated maritime onlookers often referred to the Bank Line as a tramp operator, but the truth was more complicated. A typical voyage could consist of passages in world wide Liner trades, stitched together with charters arranged at the Baltic Exchange in London, and true tramping voyages. This pattern strengthened as time went by, and worked very

The 4 masted Barque "Beechbank", after launching on the Clyde 1892. She went on to sail for 32 years with Bank Line and subsequent owners, before being scrapped. A remarkable sailing ship achievement.

successfully for more than 100 years.

Orders for the first steamships were given to the Russell & Co yard, and it was a characteristic of Bank Line buildings over the years that batches were ordered. It is an impressive list, i.e. Single ships were first ordered, namely

'Duneric' and the 'Elleric', presumably to test the water, and then came:-

1898. 4 vessels ordered and named Boveric, Comeric, Foreric, and Gymeric.

1901 2 vessels - Tymeric and Katanga

1901. 2 vessels - Inveric and Jeseric

1905. 3 vessels - Aymeric,Boveric(2) and Yoseric

1906. 4 vessels - Suveric,Kumeric,Luceric, and Orteric.

1919. 3 vessels - Luceric (2) Comeric (2), and Orteric (2)

1919. 7 vessels - Aymeric(2), Tymeric (2), Yoseric(2), Haleric, Elveric, Foreric, and War Burman

Additionally, many more steam driven vessels were added to the fleet above over these years, which did not carry the Eric suffix as they were purchased from the

The 'Bovoric' of 1898, the third steamer to join the fleet.

yards as opportunities came up . Andrew Weir gathered a reputation for taking full advantage of marked down prices and 'too good to miss' sales, and of course he was not alone in this. Some 22 vessels with differing names in addition to the above list were added to the fleet up to 1924, and a careful study shows the opportunistic nature of the commercially aggressive owner, as ships were rapidly bought and sold. The factors at play were the time honoured ones of market forces, ship prices, finance opportunities, and fluctuating freight rates. Andrew Weir firmly believed also in supporting British yards. Successful owners had to be mentally nimble, and shrewd enough to make more right calls than bad ones. Having the right type and size of vessel, one that offered the the optimum space and reliability, coupled with economy of operation was crucial. Some 80 year later, when Bank Line and a host of other traditional British companies went into decline and oblivion, it could be argued that the owners and their Boards were unable to exhibit these rare qualities sufficiently well to survive.

A move into oil engines also came in 1924, when Harland and Wolff Ltd in Govan, received a massive order from the Bank Line for 18 twin screw ships starting with the Inverbank, and which became the class name. Andrew Weir believed strongly in oil engines as the future, and put his belief into practice with this order. Of the total, 8 vessels were to clock up over 30 years service circling the globe endlessly, another 8 were war casualties, and the Forresbank was lost in November 1958 near Port Elizabeth, South Africa, after 33 years service! The enquiry revealed that the oil settling tank in the engine room had overflowed due to the lid being open. The oil then spilt on to the hot engine exhaust manifold and the subsequent fire caused the crew to abandon ship, when she then drifted ashore. Fortunately, a rescue was effected and there were no serious casualties. Some 50 years later, the binnacle was spotted adorning a fish restaurant nearby!

In 1929 an order was placed for a further 4 ships, this time from Workman Clarke (1929) Ltd, Belfast. These were single screw ships of 5060 tons gross, the names being Deebank, Trentbank, Forthbank, and Lindenbank. The Deebank was sold out of the fleet in 1955, but served another 16 years under other owners. The Trentbank was a war casualty, and the Lindenbank stranded in 1939 on Arena Island.

Just one year after this order, in 1930, Workman Clarke again received an order for 4 further vessels, but this time they were to be twin screwed. The names were Irisbank, Lossiebank, Taybank, and Tweedbank. All four went through world war 2, and they ,gave over 30 years service each, a testament to the, designers, builders, and of course the crews that carried out this marathon service. These multiple orders between 1924 and 1930 were the backbone of the fleet for many years, and the ships came to be be regarded as maritime ' work horses' by many. A characteristic of their design was lattice type derricks, deck houses abeam of the masts, wood sheathed decks, open rails, and steam winches. They had the reliable radial davits of the day. Conditions on board were close to primitive, especially in the post war period, when life at sea was rapidly improving. The company kept the facilities adequate, but hand pumped water, and steam heated baths were common well into the 1950's.

1930 saw a further order for 2 twin screw vessels similar to the Irisbank class but this time with 8 cylinder 4 stroke engines. They were the Foylebank and the Laganbank, the latter ship unfortunately lost on the Maldives, 8 years later.

Then came an order in 1934 for 3 passenger vessels to run between Calcutta and South Africa on what became the India Natal service. They were twin screw ships with white hulls, which earned them the name of the Bank Line ' White Ships'. Called Isipingo, Inchanga, and Incomati, after town's and a river in South Africa, they were a great success carrying 50 first class passengers, 20 second class, and 500 deck passengers, often pilgrims or crew being positioned for other companies.

In 1943, the Incomati was torpedoed off Lagos with the loss of one life, but the two remaining vessels ran until 1964 when they were scrapped. Over the years, the passenger numbers were reduced and the number of lifeboats went down from 12 to 8 in accordance with the new certification. In their hey day they were a popular way for ex pat. families and their relatives to travel, with transit ports at Colombo and Durban, and they were small enough to have a yacht like atmosphere with high quality cabins and fittings. The fresh water baths they offered for the passengers was a novelty in 1939!

A single ship, the Tynebank was built in 1934 by John Readhead and Sons Ltd, at South Shields, and it was the time of the depression. She was consequently built slowly. Then, just pre war, 3 vessels were ordered from Harland and Wolff again. They were the Ernebank, Araybank, and the Shirrabank with the last two being completed in the war. The Araybank was bombed and sunk in 1941, but her sister ships made it to the breakers yard in 1963.

Post world war 2, and like many British shipping companies, a number of Liberty ships entered the fleet, after being purchased from the government. Altogether, Andrew Weir's Bank Line ran 13 so called ' Sam boats', with 12 of them taking the Bank suffix. They were completely different from the usual ships of the fleet in

many respects, probably the biggest difference being the crewing arrangements. Built with the accommodation centrally around the engine room and with a galley included in the block, the company chose to use European crews. In practice this meant men from the shipping ' pool ' that was maintained at the ports, and although

The S.S. Kelvinbank shortly after stranding on the remote Ocean Island in January 1953. Although refloated she then fouled a previous wreck from 1926, the S.S. Ooma and was then abandoned. She split just abaft of the engine room and was pounded to pieces by the sea and swell.

many fine seamen were available, the random nature of hiring inevitably led to some very disruptive voyages. There were drunken scenes, and many losses from the crew as men chose the good life ashore in Australia and New Zealand. Jobs were readily available in the 1950's when the Liberty's were in the fleet. It was not unusual in these years to return to the UK after a long voyage and the crew were all or nearly all replacements, as the original crew had fled ashore. Life on board was never dull on these voyages. Crewing reverted to the more reliable and docile Asian crews after the demise of the Liberty ships. The American build showed through in the ship design and fittings, for although the original ship design was a British one, the USA build meant that everything was noticeably to a higher standard. Bunks were wider, solid wood was used where slats would normally have been employed for bunk boards etc, and the fittings were generally chunkier. The central heating was powerful, and the steam engine below was a reliable 3 cylinder one reminiscent of a huge ' Tonka Toy '.   They were a joy to sail on for many of the officers and crew, and they served the company well. The Liberty 'Kelvinbank' was lost after grounding at Ocean Island in 1953, but the others continued to serve other lines long after they had been sold out of the fleet.

In addition to the Liberty ships, 1945 saw the addition of 3 Empire ships renamed as Etivebank, Lochybank, and Shielbank.   These were single screw vessels that were sold out of the fleet in 1955 and 56 relatively early after 10 year or so of service, the versatility of this design not being as great as purpose built vessels.

Post war, a rebuilding programme began in earnest.   First came 3 sisters in 1948 from the Doxford, Sunderland yard, given names from the cardinal points of the Compass, Eastbank, Westbank, and Southbank.   These were single screw shelter deck vessels 444ft long, with deeptanks for oil cargoes, and a 4 cylinder opposed piston Diesel engine gave a speed of near 14 knots.   These vessels were ideal for the Bank Line Pacific island trades, loading general cargo and lubricating oils out to Australasia, and often returning to the UK after sailing around the Pacific island chains loading Copra and coconut oil.   Although they served this route throughout their lives, many voyages became longer as the vessels were conveniently positioned for other commitments to Asian, African, or South American ports, thus extending the time away.   For those on board, it was a tantalising time, expecting to return to the UK after 4 to 6 months but with no guarantees! Of the three, the Southbank was lost at Washington Island in 1964, and the Westbank had a narrow escape when she was successfully towed off a beach on the island of Juan De Nova in 1952.   The Bank Line had coincidentally lost the barque ' Fernbank' at the same location back in 1902.

Next came a six ship order from Harland and Wolff, again in 1953. They were apparently modelled on the success of the previous Doxford design, although slightly larger six cylinder engines were specified. The ships were called

Beaverbank, Laganbank, Nessbank, Fleetbank, Cedarbank, and Foylebank, and they all served the company well for around 20 years before being sold on to other owners.

M.V. Ashbank one of a 17 ship order from Harland and Wolff Ltd in Belfast. Delivered in 1959. She inaugurated the first sailing from the Continent to the Pacific after years during which outward journeys were always in ballast.

In the late fifties, William Doxford received a massive order for 21 ships, both open and closed shelterdeck vessels, but all with deeptanks in the almost traditional design that the company favoured. These were delivered between 1957 and 1964 The names were: Firbank, Riverbank, Northbank, Birchbank, Streambank, Teakbank, Wavebank, Yewbank, Willowbank, Larchbank, Lindenbank, Weirbank, Testbank, Inverbank, Forresbank, Trentbank, Oakbank, Rowenbank, Laurelbank, Hollybank, and Sprucebank. They all served between 18 and 20 years approx before being sold on, with the exception of the Trentbank which was lost off Alexandria after a collision 2 years after she was completed. The Lindenbank fell victim to the tricky business of loading offshore in Fanning Island, in the Pacific where the water is too deep to anchor, and was wrecked in August 1975.

About the same time as the Doxford order, Harland and Wolff in Belfast received a further 17 ship order which ran from 1957 to 1964. These were the Cloverbank, Crestbank, Carronbank, Dartbank, Garrybank, Minchbank, Rosebank,

Ashbank, Pinebank, Elmbank, Avonbank, Levenbank, Springbank, Olivebank,Lossiebank, Roybank, and Waybank. Most of these vessels had an uneventful life, and were sold out of the fleet after 13 to 15 years, but the Levernbank stranded in southern Peru in 1973 after 12 years service, and was a total loss.

A handsome pair of larger ships were ordered in 1962 from the new Swan Hunter yard. They were the Speybank and the Marabank, each 486 ft long and around 6000 tons gross, quickly followed by an 11 ship order, 6 of which went to William Doxford in Sunderland, and 5 built by Harland and Wolff in Belfast. These were bigger 15,900 ton dwt ships of over 500 ft in length, and fitted out with deeptanks

and a 50 ton derrick, giving them versatility. The names were,Taybank, Tweedbank, Beechbank, Ernebank, Shirrbank, Teviotbank, Hazelbank, Irisbank, Nairnbank, Maplebank and Gowenbank. The latter ship had the dubious honour

Four new vessels from William Doxford & Sons Ltd in Sunderland, part of a big 21 ship order in 1957. They are the Oakbank, TaybanK, Weirbank, and Lindenbank, the latter destined to be wrecked in 1975 at Fanning Island, a regular remote Bank Line Pacific call.

of being the last Bank Line ship to be built at Belfast, ending a spectacular long run of highly successful additions to the fleet.   Then came a 12 ship order in 1972, again from Doxford. Looking at the ever growing need to lift containers, these orders then began to reflect this demand.   The ships got bigger and modified as part container ship, with a modest 192 teu container capacity. Tonnage was up again to 16,900 dwt. The ships carried the traditional names of Fleetbank, Cloverbank, Birchbank, Beaverbank, Cedarbank, Firbank, Streambank, Riverbank, Nessbank, Laganbank, Crestbank, and Fenbank. A new design allowed for 4 hatches on the forepart with the accommodation moved aft so only number 5 hatch was at the after end. The builder provided 6 cylinder oil engines. They mostly had uneventful lives and were sold on after only a relatively short   stay in the Bank Line fleet, the Laganbank going after only 3 years.

Swan Hunter Shipbuilders Ltd, South Shields, then got a valuable 6 ship order in 1973. Called the Corabank class after the lead ship, they were designed to carry 240 teu's. and had 11 oil tanks for the Pacific trade. Tonnage was 15,500 dwt, and the names were Corabank, Meadowbank, Forthbank, Moraybank, Ivybank, and Clydebank.   These were relatively successful ships, designed as they were for the growing importance of the Pacific Islands trade.

Next up were the 'Fish' class of vessels, a new naming sequence.   None of these fine vessels made it into even 10 years service, as the trades became more difficult and efforts were made to form joint ventures and liaisons which would provide some stability.   The company management and ownership went through changes occasioned by the death in 1975 of the Lord Inverforth, Morton Weir, son of the founder.   Only 7 years later in 1982, his son Roy

also died suddenly at the age of 50 in 1982 and was succeeded by his brother the Hon. Vincent Weir. Roy had inherited the title and was the hand on the tiller from 1975.

The new Fish class ships from Sunderland Shipbuilders Ltd. were given the names, Roach, Pike, Dace, Rudd, Trout and Tenchbank.   The container capacity was upped to 372 teu each, and the ships were given a design speed of 16.5 knots. On launching they were intended for a new USA/South Africa service, but this was abandoned in 1987, and the ships sold.   They were the last of the orders for Bank Line ships in batches, and it marked the end of a 100 year run of extraordinary success.   A final ship, appropriately given the name Willowbank, the same as the first vessel, was ordered in 1980 from Smith's dock in Middlesbrough, and had a container capacity of 768 teu. to participate in the ill fated Bank and Savill Line to Australasia mentioned earlier.   It was a difficult trade due mainly to the mix of containers, the need for ' dead heading' the empty units, and the awkward mix resulting from the island trades.   The financial implications can only be guessed at.

. The 1980's therefore marked a downturn in activity, and this appears to be from a variety of factors, the biggest probably being the direction and commitment to shipping itself.   The Bank Line were not alone. A cataclysmic change hit the world wide dry cargo shipping scene overturning centuries of established trades and practices, and although valiant efforts were made to introduce novel solutions, the decline was on.   In 1977 Bank and Savill Line came into being, a part container service to Australasia and the Pacific, and this struggled before it morphed into ANZDL (Australia New Zealand Direct Line) in 1984, and was then terminated in 1989, the same year that Andrew Weir Shipping was formed to bring together all of the Group's shipping activities.   There were other services such as the SafBank Line from 1979 to 1987, but the true unique world wide liner services with a large fleet of ships were gone forever.   The numbers declined rapidly as ships were disposed of, some after only a few years.

Looking back over the years, and viewed from well into the 21st century, the picture is one of accelerated growth and success during the lifetime of the founder.   New buildings and acquisitions forged ahead, almost in a frenetic way in the good times, reflecting the favourable trading conditions and the finance opportunities.   The post war building programme, extending into the 1950's , 60's , and 70's was exceptional, and it was a heady time for loyal and diligent company deck officers. They could expect to be in command of their own, often new, or near new ship, roaming the world well before they were 30.   It wasn't to last, and a view can, and perhaps should be taken, that business is business however, and opportunities are not limited to perpetuating a shipping empire.   For the many hundreds of seafarers, and the incurable romantics among us, the passing of such companies is a matter of regret.   We are left with nostalgic memories, a fine history, and from those that served on board, a sense of gratitude that the opportunity to sail the world came along when it did.

During his lifetime, Andrew Weir became the Lord Inverforth of Southgate, London in 1919 and he was accorded many honours.   During world war 1, the Government had made him Surveyor-General of supply for the Army, following a detailed report he had prepared with recommendations. This led directly to his title after the war ended.

Although the Bank Line was the heart of the shipping empire, other shipping ventures, such as a French subsidiary, and a 50% share with the Danish East Asiatic Company to own United Baltic Company were made. One major venture was into Insurance.

In summary, it was a magnificent achievement for a young man, full of ambition and gifted with considerable business acumen to build up a major British shipping enterprise with it's network of Agents and subsidiary companies. At the core of this empire was the Bank Line. His expertise saw a successful transition from sail to steam, commonly acknowledged to have been a giant maritime hurdle at that time, and one at which many others fell.   Working on into his 90th year, and dying peacefully at home in 1955, Andrew Weir's passing was too early in history for him to face the challenge of the container revolution with all his vigour. Who knows how this other great Maritime hurdle of the last 100 years, namely the rush to containerise trades,   would have been met? The virtual demise of the company instead can be viewed sadly, or perhaps even philosophically along the lines that all good things must come to an end. Certainly, Bank Line was not alone in succumbing to the huge challenges of the container revolution. It spawned many giant consortia in a world wide fanfare of publicity, often borne out of desperation. Looking back, it is clear that the last 50 years have been a catalogue of unlikely mergers and unholy alliances often between fierce shipping rivals as they struggle to stay in business, often unsuccessfully.   The saying ' Big fish eat little fish ' has never been more apt than in the maritime world. Financial consequences aside, one major sacrifice made by those shipping lines eagerly joining shipping consortia, has been the blurring or loss of their treasured and time honoured identity, something which Andrew Weir and his successors fought to preserve.

How the sea loving romantic in all of us might also prefer fading away, as opposed to the hard headed business approach of ' survival at all costs !

Appendix 2 - The Pacific Island Love Affair

For 50 years or more, before containerisation took over, Bank Line romped around the South Pacific Ocean, collecting coconuts (Copra) and coconut oil, for the home run back to Europe. This trade, idyllic to many both inside and outside of the company, came at a cost. Post war, several vessels came to grief on coral ridges, and others had a lucky escape and freed themselves, sometimes with the aid of other company ships or usually the U. S. Coastguard. Losses were minimal when compared to the huge number of uneventful voyages home, but by nature the remote locations and the primitive struggles to free themselves led to some garish press coverage. " Pacific Paradise for castaways" was one newspaper headline, after survivors were photographed waving from a beach. This danger to the ships arose because of the need to approach the islands close enough for surf boats to deliver cargo, often just a few cables from the shoreline. The normal practice of safe anchoring was not an option due to the very sharp rise of the seabed upwards.

The cargo homewards of Copra was loose in the holds and consisted of coconut flesh, i.e. the white meat from the inside, which had been dried either by the sun naturally, or in a kiln. The kernels, some nearly whole, but mostly broken into pieces, were very dusty and came with a strong and distinctive smell. It also was accompanied by the small black tenacious Copra bug which got everywhere on the ship, and in particular in the baked bread. Clouds of these bugs would congregate around the hatch corners inside folds of the tarpaulins, and they were also attracted to the heat of the galley - hence their presence in batches of bread.

Bank line's Pacific loadings started way back at the turn of the century when both the sailing ships and early steamers would load bagged Copra in spare hold spaces after leaving Australia. The first full cargo however was recorded in 1922 and was from Rabaul in New Britain to Hamburg, Germany. Early cargoes then went mainly to Marseilles and Rotterdam in regular bi-monthly sailings. Close involvement with the many islands and their economy led to Bank Line ships appearing on postage stamps issued by Pacific nations. The one pictured here of the Olivebank was issued by Tuvalu, formally the Ellis Islands.

Post WW2, the big fleet of old and new tonnage was employed in trading worldwide, but the involvement in the Island loading of Copra enabled the vessels to return back to Europe and it was always the passport to a shorter trip if appointed to one of these ships. The vessels mainly returned home with Copra or if not, were fixed on a voyage charter from the open market. Grain or maybe iron or manganese ore were common cargoes to European ports. The most regular port and frequent destination for the Copra was Birkenhead and the Lever

Bros factories served by Bromboro Dock. This dock has long gone. Some cargoes also went to other UK ports and to European ports for discharge. The Copra was processed by crushing, and the resulting oil used in many and varied applications from soap to lotions. The residue in cake form was an important animal feed.

This Island trade from the Pacific Islands was therefore an important part of the global pattern operated by the big fleet of around 50 ships, and the period under review here concerns mainly the post war boom up to the 80's during which hundreds of voyages were made. Until 1960 no regular outward loadings from the

UK or Continent were available which meant ballast voyages outwards. These are anathema to ship owners.   Around 1960, a contract was gained to ship coke to the smelting plants in New Caledonia, and offered a chance to have a neat two way trade, out to the Pacific Islands and back with Copra and oil, plus smaller quantities of expeller and by products.   A heavier base cargo like ingots was also usually involved.

 These trips were long before the advent of Global Positioning and Satellite Navigation, and the Pacific Ocean was a huge remote area, hard to comprehend. Sightings of yachts were rare, and if seen, the cause of much celebration and hospitality if in port.   Within a few years, everything changed, and large numbers of yachts, mainly from the USA, meant that even remote islands were full up and had to refuse entry to yachts except in emergency. Such were the numbers venturing out into the wide beyond.

  Ports in Samoa, Tonga, Fiji, The Line Islands, New Guinea, The Solomon Islands, and Rabaul, in East New Britain, were regularly called at.   Berths alongside were rare, but anchorages abounded. When a berth was on offer, it could often be very primitive, with trees as bollards.   A well known berth

in Rabaul for many years was the levelled deck of a WW2 Japanese ship, inevitably known as the wreck berth.   The stevedores there, mostly Australian, were heavy drinkers, and ship visits signalled party time for those on board.   In the 1950's it was also common to see the after effects of WW2, with aluminium planes in the high up jungle glinting in the sun, and many maritime wrecks dotted around.   Small Islands such as Samarai in Papua New Guinea were also a regular call for Copra.

   Up in the Line islands, a resident manager at Fanning Island, now Tabuaeran, part of the Kiribati islands, oversaw the collection and drying of the Copra and arranged for the surf boats to bring out bags in slings ready for slitting on deck and bleeding down into the holds.   The workers themselves were brought up on the ship from neighbouring Islands and slept under tarpaulins slung over the derricks on deck.   It was all very primitive, and contrasts sharply with today, when cruise ships call regularly at the same island which now has a population of some 2,500 people, and an airstrip.

In those early days, loading was slow and spasmodic with sacks of Copra handled one by one, and the ships company had time to enjoy the Pacific Islands and all

they had to offer. The crystal clear water, where fish could be seen taking the bait, and the abundance and variety of fish was but one attraction. The slow life style, the happy-go-lucky locals, the music and partying could all add up to a very seductive atmosphere.   Some officers were even known to adopt the LavaLava form of dress, which is a wrap around male skirt,

worn in Samoa and other islands, and for them to sleep ashore in the huts raised from the ground! ' Going Bush' was the phrase commonly used to describe such behaviour. On these occasions it wasn't difficult to imagine the temptations that led the men to rebel in the infamous ' Mutiny on the Bounty'!   Evening time on board after loading often meant impromptu singing by the natives accompanied and aided by some beer from the ships bond.   These sessions could be very captivating, and among the native songs, would be the famous Isa Lei or Fiji farewell song which inspired the writing of 'Now is the hour' and which became a worldwide hit. The advent of Spotify and other streaming music channels today

enables these haunting tunes to be easily recaptured, by nostalgic ex Bank Liners, like the author.

Loading Copra at anchor

Now a modern town with tourist hotels and all the trappings, Apia was another charming and idyllic call.   It was the home and resting place of Robert Louis Stevenson. The town was just emerging into the modern world back in the 50's.

A Bank Line ship loading Copra in the islands

Money was being introduced for the first time, and it was such a novelty that the one taxi in the town was used for joy riding with wages that had little meaning to the ship workers! Most were self sufficient. A ship call here left a lasting impression.

Bankline lost vessels lost in other parts of the world, but the post war Pacific losses were, Kelvinbank 1953, Southbank 1964, Levernbank 1973, and Lindenbank, 1975. Additionally, there were groundings where King Neptune was narrowly cheated, such as the Beaverbank in 1959, and the 1961 built

KELVINBANK

The first of the vessels in trouble post war was the liberty ship, S.S. Kelvinbank. She was one of a dozen ' Sam Boats' that Andrew Weir ran and then purchased after the war. Unlike the vessels that were caught on coral when loading Copra, she touched bottom just after loading a full cargo of phosphate rock at Ocean

Island in January 1953. She had finished loading from the moorings, and set sail only to take the ground at Sydney Point, nearby. The vessel freed herself, but then ran foul of a previous wreck, the Ooma of 1905. It was really bad luck, but fouling the tail shaft and propeller of the old wreck did for the Kelvinbank which quickly broke up under the pounding of the open sea. A Sydney report of the time stated:

"Pinned by an 18in. steel shaft to the wreck of a steamer lost at Ocean Island in 1936, the 7,269 ton British freighter Kelvinbank is a total loss.

A marine salvage expert, Capt. J. W. Herd, told this strange story when he returned to Brisbane after his attempt to salvage the Kelvinbank, which grounded at Sydney Point, on the island, in January. Sea

and tide had driven the propeller and shaft of the old ship, the Oomah, 50ft. into the hull of the Kelvinbank, he said.

"We had her floating, but it was impossible to free her," said Captain Herd. "When I left Ocean Island 12 days ago the Kelvinbank was breaking up."

 Both Ocean Island and Nauru were regular loading islands for Bank Line on behalf of the British Phosphate Commission, and these small remote islands close to the equator offered a taste of Island life, different from the Copra ports. Heavy surface mining had pock marked the surface, but on Ocean Island, a level patch provided a games field where the ships crew could be asked to play both cricket or football. A novelty on the cricket pitch was the outfield where balls disappeared into the deep crevices formed by surface mining. These matches were held against the resident phosphate commission staff ashore.   Nauru had the advantage of a loading gantry which speeded up the loading prior to a 10 day trip down to Australian or New Zealand ports through the Tasman Sea. On Ocean Island, giant buckets were still used.

BEAVERBANK

The Beaverbank, a regular ship that had made dozens of voyages around the islands came to grief in July 1959. She was freed miraculously without major damage from the reef in English Harbour at Fanning Island, now part of Kiribatu, but not before all the valuable coconut oil had been pumped out into the Pacific

Ocean. With no vessels or tanks to receive the oil, it was pumped overside, and an aerial picture taken at the time shows a huge white lake surrounding the ship as the oil solidified. Copra was also jettisoned, and finally the assisting vessel sent from Hawaii managed to free her. This was the USS Current, and the British RFA Fort Beauharnois assisted. A lengthy report later by the U.S. Navy included some interesting information and highlighted the extensive salvage operations. Shortly after grounding, 2280 tons of bunkers and coconut oil were pumped overboard, which only allowed the vessel to move further inwards to the beach. 900 tons of Copra was also laboriously jettisoned. It then became necessary to ballast down, and some 3300 tons of salt water ballast was added to hold the ship steady until a salvage attempt could be made. The master signed a Lloyds 'No cure - No pay' salvage form, and operations commenced. She was finally freed on the 24th July 1959, surprisingly with only some hull plating and bilge keel damage, and managed to steam away without further assistance.

Beaverbank ashore and dumping Copra

Other vessels of the fleet had contact with the coral over the years, but details are scarce, especially as records only dwell on losses. One incident that was talked about in the company involved the 1967 built Maplebank, which grounded at full speed during a passage from Suva to Lautoka when loading oil and copra. Tiredness played a part it seems, after spending all day loading and then carrying out watches at night. Fortunately she

was freed on a spring tide, using an old hulk that was sunk in a suitable place to get a purchase and haul off.

SOUTHBANK

In 1964, on Boxing Day, the 1948 built M.V. Southbank, a regular Copra ship ran into serious trouble when she drifted on to coral at Washington Island, a remote part of the Line Islands in the Pacific. She touched bottom in the swell, and quickly broke in two aft

of the accommodation. The remoteness of the Line Islands, 1200 miles south of Hawaii, made rescue attempts for the survivors difficult. The US Navy and Coastguard, based in Hawaii proved crucial, and they literally came to the rescue. Their specialist vessel ' Winnebago' picked up Southbank survivors, but not before some of the wives and younger officers had become attracted to the surroundings and lifestyle. The islanders looked after the castaways, preparing breakfasts and showing them the island way of living. However, the loss was marked by the sad death of the

Southbank survivors waiting for rescue

young second mate, who was killed returning to the ship shortly after she was abandoned. Everyone got safely on the beach, but it was decided to send a return party to pick up island mail and other items, and a huge wave smashed the boat alongside. A first hand account later by one of the officers gives a dramatic glimpse of the moments after the ship struck....

" When we got to Washington Island we had been loading Copra for about a week steaming in on the ebb tide and drifting out while still loading. We had the usual Christmas dinner and drinks etc. The next day we ran aground. The ship was sort of juddering, and I got out of bed and as the juddering got worse, I realised we were aground.

I shot out in boiler suit and desert boots onto the after deck, past the galley, to the engine room door. The noise was bedlam, and the deck was heaving up. At the door I met the engine room crew bailing out. They were panicking and I shouted at them to ' blankety blank' get back. Managed to get them down to the plates, but was then told to send them out as it looked bad.   The whole main engine was heaving up and down about 12 inches. The 6 thousand psi relief valves were overloaded and going off, and when it is 8 of them it is sheer bedlam.   I was sent down the tunnel to sound the tanks, and when I started further down to get to number 6, the tunnel walls started to collapse around me. I got out like a rocket and saw the Second Engineer talking on the phone.   The phone cord was stretching as he spoke due to the R.S.J. pole to which it was fixed bending like a candy bar.   We then got the abandon ship signal, and I went to my cabin for a bag with a few things and then up to

Southbank Breaking up

the boat deck.   The boats were still in their chocks, but the crew were all sitting in them! Anyway, we got them lowered and headed for the shore.   On shore everyone was milling around and it was decided to go back to collect mail and other items. The weather was beautiful, with only a 2 meter swell. Little did I know what was to transpire. "

Then follows a sad description of the tragic accident mentioned above, the life ashore on the island, and the experience of the rescue by the USS Winnebago which lifted back the survivors to Honolulu and thence home.

LEVERNBANK

The next casualty to occur in the Pacific Ocean was the Levernbank, but this time the culprit was fog.   Fully loaded with general cargo, she stranded on the Peruvian coast at Matarani in 1973.   The ship managed to get free and float away but she was fatally damaged and sank later.   Another first hand report from one of the engineers gives his experience as the vessel struck…..

"I was on watch with the 3rd Engineer at the time the ship struck rocks around 3am.   The propeller also hit rocks and it wrapped the blades around the propeller and this took the main engine out, so that was it. Within what seemed like seconds the crew were into their paying off suits, jackets stuffed with cartons of

fags, and ready for the off. We had loaded on the Bay of Bengal West Coast of S.America service, and had the normal run up the coast after the Straits of Magellan, calling at Punta Arenas, Valparaiso, Antofagasta, and a host of smaller ports. We had radar problems which were

supposed to be fixed at a stop in Durban, but which started again as soon as we left port.   As I recall, Matarani would not accept vessels at night, so the plan was to stop and drift as anchoring was not possible due to the depth of water.   As we tracked up the coast there seems to have been an underestimation of our distance off, and as we turned, progress was interrupted by a 'bump' which at first I thought was a fishing boat, but which in fact was our first contact with the Peruvian mainland. The engines were still at ' Full Ahead ' at this time. The we got ' Stand by ' followed by a double ring ' Full Astern ' and then a major BANG and the engine stopped dead. I ran down the tunnel to see the tail shaft out of line and the last two bearing pedestals tipped over about 30 degrees. I reported this to the second who considered the best thing to do was to put the kettle on!

When dawn broke, we were inside of a small cove, and was a perfect fit - couldn't have got in there if we wanted to. The cove or islet, I suppose was surrounded by high cliffs, upon which stood several of the locals 'taking the Michael'. A tug was sent out from the port and promptly turned the wrong way. A couple of distress rockets soon had it coming our way. The tug then towed us out to deep water where we assessed damage and attempted to keep the ship afloat in the vain hope that assistance was a realistic prospect. It wasn't. The ship was abandoned by the help of the small anchovy fishing boats around. We had an enforced stay in Peru while our status was sorted out and then we were repatriated home. "

LINDENBANK

Soon after losing the Levernbank, the company suffered the loss of the Lindenbank. Built 1961, she was lost at Fanning Island in August 1975 after grounding on the reef. Strenuous efforts were made at salvage, and another company ship, the Elmbank assisted, but to no avail. Once again, the US Navy also attempted to assist, and they despatched USS Bolster and USS Brunswick, but the damage had been done. Lindenbank pumped out all of the oil cargo, causing a growing environmental protest, but the ship was pivoting on a pinnacle of coral, and soon broke her back. A wreck report held in March 1977 stated....

"The Lindenbank was manned at the time by a crew of 59 hands all told. At the time of the casualty she was laden with a general cargo including island produce and vegetable oils of a weight of 8,700 tons consigned to the United Kingdom and Continent. The vessel sailed from Christmas Island on 14 August 1975 bound for Fanning Island in the Line Islands, and she arrived off English Harbour in Fanning Island at about 0800 local time on 15 August. Here she was to load copra and cargo operations began about 0930. Inside English Harbour it was too shallow for the Lindenbank to anchor: outside it was too deep. Following the practice of similar sized vessels the Lindenbank drifted off the island to load cargo from surf boats, frequently adjusting her position to give maximum lee to the surf boats. At

the end of the day's loading she was allowed to drift seaward in a north-westerly direction. " It goes on to censure the Master and the third Officer, for the subsequent grounding in English Harbour.

"We censure the Master for not checking accurately the Radar position, when Lindenbank was only 1 1/2 miles off English Harbour. The Radar position was made by an uncertificated Acting Third Mate. The Master left no written or even verbal instructions to check the vessel's position at least every 1/4 hour and to call him if the vessel was closing land. We appreciate his honesty and forthright acceptance of blame and have had such in mind. " The court also made a statement as follows :-

" New or old, a proper look out must be kept AT ALL TIMES (see M Notice No 756). This disaster clearly shows the vital need for Night Orders to be made by all Masters for the guidance of navigational watch keepers. This is especially important where the navigational watch keeper is uncertificated. In an age of science, when navigational aids increase, human skills must not be overlaid. The sea will catch the unwary who are not ready for the unexpected or unpredicted. "

So said the court. The conclusion was not something that a reasonable person might quarrel with, but most navigators would shudder hearing those words which were a version of stating the obvious.

In the break bulk years, when cargo was still handled loose, either in boxes, bundles, drums, or sometimes on pallets, an appointment to a Copra ship for the Mates, and for the Apprentices, spelled a familiar routine. If necessary all of the fleet could be pressed into the homeward carriage of Copra, but the route suited those vessels with a good deep tank capacity. These tanks were great for liquid, but more often than not they were also used for bulk cargo. Some ships, notably the 'Compass' class and their successors were perfect, mainly because the deep tanks provided ample capacity for oil, and loading home was fine tuned so that the vessels were both full and down to their marks when leaving the load ports. This was achieved by having a base cargo of lead or copper ingots from Northern Queensland, Cairns or Townsville, usually around the 4000 ton mark. This went in the lower holds, later to be topped up by copra. (After the Southbank stranded, and some 9 years later, the lead ingots in her holds were the subject of a salvage attempt by the trans Pacific rower, John Fairfax, who had stopped off at Washington Island on his amazing rowing feat, and he had spotted the opportunity then.) Valuable coconut oil filled the tank spaces, and the job was done. This vegetable oil needed twice daily checks for leaks and temperature. If all went well, steam heating kept the oil suitably liquid to enable the pumping to take place through pipes, often to road tankers at the discharge port. It was common to join a ship in winter in the UK, and the white oil had solidified down the ships side, much like candle grease. This occurred if a leak ran from joints in the pipe. A distinctive aroma, chiefly of coconut instantly filled the surrounding air and conjured up the unforgettable surroundings of the South Sea islands even if snow was on the ground!

Due to the outward leg from the U.S. Gulf ports usually involving the loading of rock sulphur in the lower holds, strict and thorough cleaning of all surfaces was a necessity, before arriving at the islands. It had to be done sufficiently

well to gain the acceptance of the load surveyor. The tanks outward bound mostly carried forms of lubricating oil, necessitating even more stringent cleaning. Steam coils were used to heat the coconut oil on the homeward leg, as it was prone to solidify. Also, the big lids on the deep tanks, secured with dozens of bolts, and with greasy cotton packing beneath the lids meant that the Mates and Apprentices were kept fully engaged throughout. Familiarity with all sorts of wrenches and spanners helped as they often struggled, through the night in many cases, wrestling with the lids to get a satisfactory tight fit. Steam cleaning prior to loading with a caustic solution was the norm. To some, the whole cycle of tank cleaning, inspection, loading, and monitoring, was a nightmare scenario, but the regular mates quickly learnt the ropes.   Voyages were 2 years, unless appointed to a ship likely to be favoured for the Copra run. It was a compensation of sorts for the tank routine. There were also familiar routes around the world that Bank Line had contracts for, such as the US Gulf ports to Australasia, and India to Africa and S America with gunnies and Jute.   Looking at a world map, a typical long voyage would include several of these ' legs' and occasionally included a ballast voyage. Positioning suitable ships was an art form.   The company boast was that a ship could be made available in almost any load port worldwide in the minimum of days, something that could only be done with a sufficiently large and widespread fleet.   It was a world wide pattern stitched together with regular liner routes and ad hoc tramping links as described. The London chartering Director and his team ably filled in these gaps with spot charters fixed on the Baltic exchange.

For the regulars who enjoyed sailing on those Bank Line round the islands services, the impact was huge.   It was anything but routine, and for some that caught the bug badly, it was life changing.   Intense star studded heavens, the balmy relaxed nights, hugely colourful and breathtaking sunrises and sunsets, and the intoxicating atmosphere around the islands, all contributed to the feeling that it was a special and somewhat privileged experience, never to be forgotten.

Other Books by the author

"Any Budding Sailors?"

"Trampship and Ferry Voyages"

"Shipwrecks and Sorrow"

website: banklineonline.com

About the author.

Born in Jersey, Channel Islands, the author left with his parents prior to the German occupation. Then followed a period in the London Blitz where he witnessed the daily damage and the anti-aircraft guns in Finsbury Park.

Following a career at sea and ashore in senior positions in the shipping industry, he is now retired in Cornwall, surrounded by family and Grandchildren. Writing, photography, and portrait painting are among his hobbies, and he has had several shipping articles published in addition to books about maritime history and a memoir called, " Any Budding Sailors?"

Printed in Great
Britain
by Amazon